4/1/14

Lawrence + Doris,

Thank you for being friends of a special kind. This book, written by our minister here in Ridge Farm, is given to you as a token of appreciation for your many years of love (agape) and friendship.

Yours for eternity,

Dick

The Surpassing Righteousness

The Surpassing Righteousness

The Sermon on the Mount for Would-be Disciples

CHARLES R. DAVIS

To order additional copies of this book, contact:
Xlibris Corporation
1-888-795-4274
www.Xlibris.com
Orders@Xlibris.com
125990

TABLE OF CONTENTS

CHAPTER 1—THE SERMON AND ITS STRATEGY

How does one begin to present something that is far from simple? How does one present ideas that few people, or perhaps no people, have ever considered? It is true that the question one begins with determines the answer one discovers. If the question is wrong or wrong-headed, the answer is likely to be wrong. This is our problem in beginning our quest for becoming disciples to the full measure of the stature of Christ. To begin by studying the Bible is not a bad place to start. In fact, if someone is considering becoming a Christian, or has decided to become one, there is no other place to begin. But where in the Bible does one begin? It is tempting to begin the way we begin all books, by starting at page 1. It is so natural to begin on page 1 that some explanation for beginning elsewhere may be required. I suggest we begin with Jesus. We will venture out from this center always with the understanding that we, like a tethered ball, are anchored at this center.

What is the center of Jesus? What lies at His core? Let's recommend a governing principle. Let's make the various competing theological views secondary to the primacy of the Bible itself. In other words, when a theological view appears to compete with something a biblical text appears to say, we should give primacy to the biblical text. Further, where two or more biblical texts appear to conflict with each other, that interpretation is preferable which compatibilizes them.

JESUS'S PROBLEM

Consider that as soon as God plans for His incarnation as Jesus of Nazareth, He accepts some conditions for the presentation of His values, plans, and

1

strategies. Those to whom He will present His plans and expectations control much of the form in which He may present them. For example, a relatively mature and educated adult with a relatively well-formed concept and value system needs to convey these things to children. But these children have a limited cognitive base that restricts the ways the adults can transmit this knowledge and these values. A very young child will not have the language of the adults, and the child will certainly not yet have the relatively sophisticated conceptual framework of the adult world. In beginning, an adult will have to present first things first. What are these first things for Jesus?

How does the process of developing a disciple begin, and to what end does it aim? Jesus has an objective for anyone who would become His disciple. Setting out what that objective is in very clear terms is necessary before Jesus can formulate His strategy for presenting these objectives. What does a disciple of Christ look like? The extent to which we fail to identify what Jesus means by "becoming a disciple" is the extent to which our disciples will fail to look like what Jesus wants. In the Sermon on the Mount, Jesus gives us a picture of what He expects of those who would be His disciples.

Consider another aspect of Jesus's problem. Jesus has no Internet, no radio or TV. He has no printing press or mass distribution capabilities. Once He specifies in His own mind what kind of people His disciples should become, He has to decide how to present these objectives to people in such a way that He can maximize their exposure within the context of the technology of His time—a technology which is, in our terms, quite primitive. The answer, given His world of presentation, is that He will have to travel around speaking to crowds in villages and cities. Given that He travels to where people are, although some will follow Him around, He will have to present the same message at each of these places. The message will have to be clear, concise, and cogent. He has three years in which to make enough of an impact to assure that the message will survive. The message will have to live on in and be transmitted inter-generationally by those who hear it from Him. This is the place of the *Sermon on the Mount* in Jesus's ministry.

Many people might allow the use of the term "sermon" to taint Jesus's objective. Preachers develop and write different sermons weekly. This they can do because they have the luxury of having the same audience for relatively long periods of time. Jesus does not have this luxury, so we err in imposing this notion on His ministry. Jesus very likely worked a very long time on the ideas in this message and honed them into a well-structured easily remembered form.

Scholars have long wondered whether the other sermon, the one in Luke, is a corruption of this one in Matthew. Some hypothesize that the differences are important indicators of the inability of disciples to copy down some static text. This is, of course, silliness. Anyone who travels around speaking to a variety of audiences in a variety of places will present similar concepts on a constant theme. But only those bereft of creativity will think that the same message is proper for any and all audiences. But, given Jesus's problem, if He wants to get a message out, the message must be consistent though the presentations need not necessarily be identical.

Comprehending the *Sermon* as a whole is important since Jesus delivered it as a whole nearly every place He went. When people heard it, they responded to its ideas after having heard it from beginning to end, perhaps multiple times. "They were amazed at His teaching, for He taught as one having authority, and not as the scribes and Pharisees." Upon reflection, this truth becomes quite clear. Think of how our society conceives of ways to repeat messages multiple times. Audio and videotaping, stenographers and manuscripts, copy machines and now digital storage and retrieval are only a few of the ways we seek to preserve profound messages.

The society Jesus worked within used a highly sophisticated biotechnology. They used the brain to remember what they heard. This may seem to be a primitive storage and retrieval system for the twenty-first century. However, there was no other efficient way to store and retrieve information than to remember it. But this skill is not subject to the vagaries of the entertaining parlor game or the pyrrhonistic educational activity. When the viability of life and truth depend on precisely remembering and recounting messages, the expectations of oral traditions become more important than they do in our world wherein we may be somewhat sloppy in recollection since we have relatively sophisticated objective media retrieval systems.

It is rather difficult for me to follow scholars who strain out gnats only to swallow camels. Why must we be unsure, as many of them say we must, of what Jesus actually said? They argue that the words of Jesus are those that made it through the agenda filter of His disciples. They say that what we have of what Jesus may have said is just *what His followers wanted to preserve* or *those things that were in their interest to preserve.* I am unsure of how these scholars can be so sure of a negative truth in support of an unfalsifiable hypothesis.

If things are as we have discussed up to now, the *Sermon on the Mount* is one of the most well-attested messages in history. Further, if those disciples who were so committed to Jesus as a person that they followed Him from village to village and city to city for three years incessantly hearing the ideas of the Sermon, it would be difficult to conceive of any mistakes at all and certainly no errors of the magnitude that the scholars press upon us.

THE SERMON ON THE MOUNT

The Sermon on the Mount is less about God's offering salvation than it is about God's setting holiness expectations. I have read and studied the *Sermon* many times—not only in English, but also in Greek. I tried to understand it within the context of the prevailing evangelical paradigm, namely that God offers salvation to people who were incapable of obeying God's Law. I have tried to understand people who keep on saying that no one can meet God's expectations and that only those who acknowledge that people cannot do it on their own are those whom God somehow enables to conform to these standards. The great enlightenment genius Erasmus asked Martin Luther, in their debate over whether or not the will was free, why there are so many commands in the Bible. Erasmus thought that giving someone a command to do or not to do something presupposed the capacity to comply with the command. Luther writes that this is not God's purpose in giving these biblical commands. According to Luther, God gave these commands so that when people tried to comply with them, they would realize their inadequacy and turn to God and rely solely on Him.[1]

There is nothing of this kind of the reasoning in the *Sermon*. Presently, I am not prepared to say that something like this kind of Reformation reasoning is not somewhere in the Bible, although I hope there is not. There may well be some conditions under which someone cannot comply with these just holiness expectations. What I am prepared to say is that Jesus says nothing of this kind in His core message. If it is absent in the core *Sermon*, it becomes appropriate to ask the question, "Why is it absent?" The Luther-

---

[1]   Martin Luther *The Bondage of the Will* [Feather Trail Press—Amazon.com, 2009] In this regard Luther gives exactly the same response as Augustine gave in responding to Caelestius in his *A Treatise Concerning Man's Perfection in Righteousness*. *Nicene and Post-Nicene Fathers*, vol. 5

like reasoning is presented as though it is at the core of the Gospel. Yet, it is clearly absent from Jesus's core message. How can this be?

If the Sermon is about anything, it is about what God justifiably expects from anyone who expects to participate in the coming Kingdom of Heaven. One's righteousness must surpass that of scribes and Pharisees.[2] One must refrain from immoral actions because of righteous character.[3] One must do righteous acts without any consideration of reward or recognition.[4] One must stop living life around wealth, either in acquiring it or wanting to acquire it.[5] Merely acting properly is morally insufficient since "not everyone who says to me 'Lord, Lord' will enter the Kingdom of Heaven, but only those who actually comply."[6] It is the wise man, not the foolish one, who enters the Kingdom of Heaven because he builds his house on the solid rock of "these words of mine," i.e., the holiness standards of the Sermon.[7]

Whereas John the Baptist focused on repenting from *doing* the things that were morally wrong, Jesus now specifies that *doing* what is right goes beyond the cessation of *doing* what is wrong. He will illustrate in both message and ministry what is morally right in both behavior and character. If the Sermon is about anything, it is about a disciple's becoming morally responsible.

Let us think for a moment about moral responsibility. First, no one can be morally responsible who cannot discern and choose to act in accordance with normative moral standards. God may justifiably set moral standards for people to the extent that the people who are expected to comply with them can, in fact, know what they are and willingly comply with them. Second, God may justifiably hold people morally responsible for not complying with these holiness standards in virtue of their capacity to comply, should they choose to comply. So God would be unjust if He held anyone morally responsible for failing to comply with holiness standards when that person could not, in fact, comply with them. Since God is not unjust, it follows that the moral standards God establishes are either within the capacity of people

---

2   Matthew 5:20

3   Matthew 5:21–48

4   Matthew 6:1–18

5   Matthew 6:19–34

6   Matthew 7:21–23

7   Matthew 7:24–27

to know what they are and do in fact comply with them, or God cannot justifiably hold them morally responsible for their failure to comply.[8] If all of this is true, then it makes sense for Jesus to set out God's expectations for holiness in the *Sermon*. It also explains why there is so little about God's offering salvation, grace, or forgiveness in the *Sermon*. Such an offer is premature since Jesus must first get people to acknowledge that they are sinners and are morally responsible for being so.

Why are we so intent on offering a solution to a problem people fail to realize they have? We may have in mind, as Luther did, to protect God's name against impudence. Unfortunately, Luther failed to see that if God consigns to eternal condemnation those people who cannot comply with the standards of holiness in virtue of which He consigns them to perdition, then God condemns people who cannot be held morally responsible. If God is all-powerful, as is commonly asserted of Him, then whether people are sinners or not is a function of God's choice, not of man's. Therefore, if there are evil people, it is due to God's indifference or indolence. It cannot be due to the moral irresponsibility of people themselves. This is not the picture of God that Jesus paints in the *Sermon*. God holds people morally responsible because they can comply with what holiness demands. The *Sermon* is about how and why God holds people morally responsible. This is also why it is the constant refrain of the prophets that people repent or face the wrath of God. Apart from volitional repentance, there can be no just salvation.

GOD'S PROBLEM

Jesus goes beyond the Old Testament. He shows the relationship of God's love and mercy, on the one hand, and His justice and goodness, on the other. Consider that once God creates people with the capacity to comply with holiness, God has no problem as long as people do, in fact, comply with His just holiness expectations. God's problem arises when free people choose to rebel against those just holiness expectations God establishes. Once rebellion occurs, God has only four logically possible courses of action open to Him.

---

8   This is the argument Pelagius presented against Augustine's theology, a theology followed by the major reformers. See: Adolf von Harnack *The History of Dogma* [New York: Dover Publications, 1961].

1. God may exercise his moral right to summarily condemn anyone and everyone who fails to comply with these just holiness expectations.
2. God may suspend the just holiness expectations in favor of universally forgiving everyone who chooses to disregard them.
3. God may arbitrarily save some moral rebels and not the others.
4. God may offer salvation and forgiveness to people who voluntarily choose to comply with just holiness standards.

What are the moral consequences of each of these four possibilities? In the first case, although God would be within His moral right to hold people responsible for their moral irresponsibility, He would not be as morally good as He could be if His character contained both the traits of moral indignation and mercy. So this option is less desirable than it might otherwise be should the character quality of mercy have no moral value. In the second case, were God to choose this option, namely that it is morally superior to exercise mercy and love at the expense of holiness, there would be no reason for people to behave according to a just holiness standard since failing or refusing to comply with it would have no moral consequence. There is a clear moral distinction between those who were relatively better in complying with the just holiness expectations and those who were relatively worse in complying with them. Yet, in exercising this second option, God would be treating both in the same way. This is not a problem unless just holiness expectations have value. If they have value, then treating these two groups the same would be unjust. *Thirdly*, one must ask whether God, or anyone else for that matter, would be just if He treated people in the same moral condition in different ways.[9] The third option holds that all people are equally sinful, but God arbitrarily chooses to save some and not others.[10] Now, of course, if God were to do such a thing, no one who was not also omnipotent could do anything about it. But having enough power

---

9   If all people are equally depraved or tainted by original sin, then all human beings are in the same moral condition.

10   These are said to be the elect of God. Their election is obviously not a function of their self-determined choices, since their choices, to the extent they have any, are morally corrupt. So, God cannot use the moral state of any person as a guide in deciding on who the elect are. Therefore, his choice is arbitrary, a function of his sovereign choice which, according to those who advocate man's moral impotence, no man may deign to question. I do call this into question in order to defend the faith against the charge of injustice.

to get away with being unjust does not make any injustice just. This is the problem with the Divine Command theory of ethics. Might does not, after all, make right—even if it is God who has the might. Since each of the first three options would contain some level of moral imperfection in God, the fourth option—to require people to repent and comply with just holiness expectations—is the most just way of offering mercy, forgiveness, or grace. In other words, it is just and merciful for God to accept the repentance commitment of people as a condition of His saving grace. It becomes the responsibility of anyone who expects to receive God's grace to comply with those holiness expectations.

JUST HOLINESS EXPECTATIONS

We have referred to "just holiness expectations," but we have not identified what they are. I will propose that there are four of them. God may justifiably expect people to comply with all four of them.

1. Every person is morally responsible for treating all people with dignity and respect since God has created all people in His image.
2. Every person is morally responsible for moral goodness in himself and others.
3. Every person is morally responsible for being an advocate for what is true, right, and good.
4. Every person is morally responsible for being proactive in the reconciliation of all people to God and to each other.

These are what are called in categorical logic "Class A" statements. If anyone is prepared to call in question any of these "Class A" just holiness expectations, then one has to be prepared to defend what in categorical logic is called a "Class O" statement. The following are the corresponding "Class O" statements for the above just holiness expectations.

1. Some people are not morally responsible for treating all people, or even some people, with dignity and respect.
2. Some people are not morally responsible for moral goodness in themselves and others.
3. Some people are not morally responsible for being advocates for what is true, right, and good.

4. Some people are not morally responsible for being proactive in the reconciliation of all people to God and to each other.

As you read through the *Sermon*, ask yourself whether Jesus presupposes these four principles of just holiness expectations. Is there any reason to suggest that Jesus would accept any one or more of those in the second set? What kind of religious or moral framework would Jesus be advocating if He were to be an advocate of the "Class O" list? Test through your study of the *Sermon* to determine whether Jesus sets out to advocate the "Class A" or the "Class O" lists.

JESUS—THE INCARNATION OF GOD

If the Christian doctrine of the incarnation means anything, it means that God became the man Jesus and limited Himself to all of the properties that human beings have. As the Hebrew writer says: "He was tempted in all points like as we are and yet was without sin."[11] Since Jesus proved in His own life that man is capable of complying with God's just holiness expectations, He also proves by His life that we who fail to comply with them are morally irresponsible sinners and that God's wrath is justified.[12] Paul agrees with this conclusion:

> No temptation has seized you except what is common to man. And God is faithful; he will not let you be tempted beyond what you can bear. But when you are tempted, he will also provide a way out so that you can stand up under it.[13]

This shift in orientation runs counter too much of prevailing evangelical theology. This Reformed view advocates that people are morally impotent and that Jesus had a way of avoiding sin in virtue of His being God's son. Apparently, the inconsistency of this belief escapes notice. If Jesus is fundamentally unlike us as human beings, then He is somehow incapable of sinning, and so cannot be tempted. But this contradicts the plain

---

11 Hebrews 4:15

12 Romans 1:18 ff

13 I Corinthians 10:13

teaching of the Hebrew writer. So either the popular belief is wrong, or the Hebrew writer is wrong. In any event, it is plainly true that both cannot be correct.

On the other hand, if people cannot help but sin because of their human nature, then it cannot be just to hold them responsible for what they do since they cannot do otherwise than sin (if it makes any sense to call their violations of just holiness expectations "sin"). As Augustine puts it: *non posse, non peccare*. "Man is not able not to sin." But this violates the clear implications of Paul's views in I Corinthians 10. Again, either the prevalent evangelical view of the sinfulness of people is wrong or else the Pauline view of people is wrong. In any case, both cannot be true at the same time. We are forced to choose between the biblical texts or the popular views. Of course, if we argue for the latter, then we have no need for the Bible. Perhaps we could supplant the Bible with the *Westminster Confession* and its catechisms. If the Bible is true, it would be a good idea to alter our beliefs to bring them into line with the Bible. In any case, the stronger moral position is the biblical one. So it should be of no surprise that Jesus and His disciples take it.

CHAPTER 2—THE DISCIPLESHIP PILGRIMAGE

I once heard that when Soren Kierkegaard was asked whether he was a Christian, he answered that he was not yet a Christian, but that he was becoming one. In the opening of the *Sermon on the Mount,* Jesus reveals that becoming a disciple of God's Kingdom is a process. It begins with the acknowledgment that one is in spiritual poverty, and it ends with the moral courage to become as holy as God justifiably expects even though one may be persecuted for having such courage.

There are many interpretations and analyses of the beatitudes. In general, each of these nine strings as segments is regarded as more or less arbitrarily arranged. They are often regarded as though each has a truth of its own, sermons devoted to each individually. I think this is a mistake. Consider that Jesus is describing the process of the personal transformation of someone who finally discovers he/she is in spiritual poverty to someone who becomes an advocate for what is true, right, and good. This is the orientation to the beatitudes that we undertake here.

"THE POOR IN SPIRIT"

Kierkegaard also wrote a book in which he discloses the characteristics of someone in despair—a condition he equates with being in sin.[14] In the course of his analysis, he distinguishes between people who are in despair and know that they are and those who are in despair and fail to realize that they are. I can think of no better commentary on this first beatitude than

---

14   Soren Kierkegaard, *Fear and Trembling and The Sickness Unto Death* Translated by Walter Lowrie [Princeton, NJ: Princeton University Press, 1941 (Reprinted 1974)]

Kierkegaard's book. Those who are in despair and yet fail to notice that they are, he says, are doubly removed from being in a position to be saved than are those who recognize their condition. These people are doubly removed from salvation because they fill the void left by the absence of holiness with trivial things like property, pleasure, power, and prestige. The other kind of person is the one who knows she/he is in despair and also knows that no amount of property, pleasure, power, or prestige can compensate for being in that condition. This person is infinitely closer to redemption than the other. Kierkegaard explains philosophically what Jesus says so elegantly, "Blessed are the spiritually impoverished, for only they can become citizens of God's Kingdom."

To embark on the pilgrimage to God's Kingdom, one must first realize that the land in which she/he now dwells is rife with poverty. The Cuban boat people provide us with a metaphor for this opening beatitude and for the progression indicated by those that follow. In order to leave a place of poverty and oppression, one must risk everything that appears to offer security and set sail on an unpredictable ocean in a less than seaworthy craft. Our metaphor falls short because this trip is not from one place to another place; it is a pilgrimage from one type of person to another. The Kingdom of God is for those who will undertake this trip of personal transformation. It is for those who will accept the responsibility for becoming as holy as God justifiably expects.

"THOSE WHO MOURN"

It is easy to see how the mourning over one's spiritual impoverishment is the next natural existential step. There can be no such mourning for those whom Kierkegaard identifies as in despair without knowing it. These may seem happy enough to those they deceive in carrying out their own deception. Once one realizes one's spiritual poverty, that his/her life values are sinful (i.e., fundamentally immoral), no other experience can occur. After accepting responsibility for having become a sinner, one must either scurry back to self-deception or experience remorse.

Accepting responsibility for having become a sinner must lead to experiencing remorse if one is to continue the pilgrimage to disciplined discipleship. This remorse may be and ought to be intense, as both Peter and Judas came to realize. Both experienced the intensity of their spiritual poverty, and both experienced the intensity of their remorse. Peter wept bitterly after the third crowing of the cock.[15] Judas's remorse drove him to find a rope and the branch of a tree.[16] Each had betrayed Christ. Each had experienced his remorse intensely. [17]

It may be considered compassionate to try to diminish this experience of remorse. It is, however, good neither for our own pilgrimage nor for anyone else's. Trying to comfort someone inappropriately creates a spiritual roadblock. To say, as many often do, "Don't worry about it" or "It's okay" is a deception, whether perpetrated by the self or well-meaning others.[18] The mourning is too important to trivialize, for the level of comfort one will come to experience is greater the more intensely the guilt is felt.

"THE MEEK"

The mourning gives way to meekness. Once the hubris of the arrogant sinner breaks down, humility replaces it. There is no room for haughtiness in a disciple's character. It is tempting in the quest for happiness to acquire as much property, pleasure, power, and prestige as possible. These provide the seductive appearance of security, but these four "Ps" lie at the core of everything sinful. Any value system that justifies the acquisition of these things relies on hubris. They can neither coexist with Kingdom values, nor can they be compartmentalized. They are incompatible with the values of the Kingdom of God.

The kingdom of this world is characterized by success in acquiring things that matter little. Of what value is a fine house on a fine property, if one lies incapacitated on a fine bed in a luxuriously adorned sickroom? Of what value is wealth if it secures only the shallow adulation of sycophants at the expense of the love of family and friends? What good is success when your children would rather be elsewhere than anywhere with you? Is your loneliness any less when—because with your confidence, competence,

---

15   Matthew 26:69–75

16   Matthew 27:1–10

17   Many of the Psalms express this phenomenon. For example, consider the 6th Psalm. Vs 3: "My bones are in agony . . . my soul is in anguish . . ." vs. 6: "I am worn out from groaning, all night long I flood my bed with weeping and drench my couch with tears."

18   This may be analogous to what is known in addiction recovery as codependency. This occurs when someone needs the other to be irresponsible in order to feel worthwhile him/ herself. This prevents the addict from accepting the responsibility for his/her addiction—a necessary first step in addiction recovery.

and success—you gather things instead of people around you? However successful this acquisition should become, it is not enough to enter God's Kingdom. It is a bit like accumulating wealth in Confederate dollars. The South is not likely to rise again. The meek shall indeed inherit the earth, and they won't care that they have!

"THOSE WHO HUNGER AND THIRST FOR RIGHTEOUSNESS"

Rather than hungering for property, pleasure, power, and prestige, the disciple hungers for justice. Whereas, under the jurisdiction of the arrogant, we are starved for justice—real starvation that is due to a steady diet of property, pleasure, power, and prestige. It is as though one tries to be nourished from a steady diet of potato chips, Twinkies, and soda. There is no dearth of food volume or calories. There is, however, a dearth of nutrients. One cannot eat and drink more of these things and improve one's health. In fact, the body only grows larger while its health deteriorates.

A disciple is characterized as having come to the place where his/her hunger is for what is true, right, and good. Yet, this hunger is not primarily for personal justice in one's personal interest. The disciple does not merely want justice for him/herself. The disciple wants justice and righteousness for everyone, everywhere, and everywhen. There is a huge difference between one who cries out for justice when she/he is the victim of injustice and one who cries out for justice and righteousness when anyone is dealt with unjustly. These latter people will come to a place and time in which their hunger and thirst will not just be satisfied; they will be engorged. Disciples will have come from being spiritually impoverished to being engorged on righteousness.

"THE MERCIFUL"

Why should the wealthy, the powerful, and the arrogant (and the arrogant need not be either wealthy or powerful) care anything about mercy? The victim can reason similarly, "Why should I be merciful to anyone when no one has been merciful to me?" In fact, anyone who is in power has little reason to be merciful, since it will do little to help him/her acquire any more property, pleasure, power, or prestige. The extent to which someone outside the Kingdom of God acts mercifully, it is to merely present an appearance of mercy.

Such acts of mercy have an agenda. Kingdom mercy is not merely an action or behavior. It is a trait of character that expresses itself in behavior.

Jesus doesn't say that those who "act mercifully" but those who "are merciful" will receive mercy. Do not fail to notice the subtlety of this point. It is the essence of hypocrisy for anyone to act in a way that is inconsistent with one's character. The deception we must avoid if we are going to become disciples to the full measure of the stature of Christ[19] is to assume that a merciful act is sufficient to characterize a merciful person. Al Capone, after all, financed soup kitchens during the Depression.

The beatitude itself is deceptively simple. Consider this. *It does not say* that a disciple *should be* merciful because she/he *has received* mercy. *Nor does it say* that a disciple will *become merciful* because she/he *has received* mercy. It says that *when* (or perhaps *as*) a disciple *becomes* merciful, she/he receives mercy. This is a serious observation. Considering things this way means that God expects people to first become merciful and, as they do, God dispenses His mercy. God, according to this reading, reads one's commitment to mercy in virtue of which He dispenses His mercy.

There is a clear expectation that those who are expected to become merciful can, in fact, become so. It is a noncoerced choice. This means God justifiably expects people to take charge of their own character development. If it were otherwise, then the existence of a merciful person is not a function of personal choice, free will, and moral responsibility, but of whether God flips their moral toggle switch. Recall our premise on the *Sermon*: viz. God justifiably expects people to accept the responsibility for becoming as holy as He is. Otherwise, God's directive to Israel—"You shall be holy because I the Lord your God am holy"[20]—makes no sense whatsoever. The verses following this statement in Leviticus prescribe the behavior of people who are as holy as God expects. None of the things God expects here or anywhere else is physically or morally impossible for any person to comply with. Receiving mercy from God attends one's becoming a merciful person.

---

19 Ephesians 4:13 "until we all reach unity in the faith and in the knowledge of the Son of God and become mature, attaining to the whole measure of the fullness of Christ." NIV This translation is inconsistent with other places in which the term "mature" is translated with the accurate term "a perfect man" [εἰς ἄνδρα τέλειον]. The KJV has it correctly translated: "till we all come in the unity of the faith, and of the knowledge of the Son of God, *unto a perfect man*, unto the measure of the stature of the fullness of Christ." The perfection of Christ is the perfection expected of all people. Paul says similarly in Colossians 1:28, "We proclaim him, admonishing and teaching everyone with all wisdom, so that we may present everyone perfect [πάντα ἄνθρωπον τέλειον] in Christ." NIV

20 Leviticus 19:2 "You shall be holy because I, the Lord your God, am holy."

This really does make a lot of sense. Dispensing inappropriate mercy is a very damaging thing to the development of moral character. It allows people to conclude that there are no significant consequences to their activities. Jesus tells a parable, which we will examine in detail at a future time, about being merciful to someone who was not himself merciful.[21] A king responded to the plea of a servant who owed him a sum that he could not possibly repay. The king forgave the debt. Afterwards, this servant threw someone into prison for an insignificant debt owed to him. When the King discovered this atrocity, he became angry and condemned the man to the same prison sentence he would have had to endure before.

The astute observer will notice an apparent incompatibility in these statements. Are the teaching of the beatitude and the teaching of this parable of the unforgiving servant at odds? In the latter case, the mercy seems to be dispensed first. In the beatitude, receiving mercy seems to depend on becoming merciful. Think about how they may be compatible. Of this much we can be sure. The spiritual pilgrimage of the disciple requires that she/he become merciful in character, not merely in actions.

"THE PURE IN HEART"

There is, as they say, none so blind as those who will not see. We have perhaps all tried to get someone to see the consequences of her/his values or lifestyle. I am a parent of two girls. It is most difficult to try to get them to see that the values they use in making life decisions will destine the future with which they will have to deal. I also teach in a prison college system. I have the reputation for being hard (perhaps "challenging" is a better word). Sometimes—although less often now than in the past, for my reputation precedes me—students will complain about how hard it is to get an A. They will whine that I should lighten up on their workload because they have only received a GED, or their high school teachers and schools were bad, or their families and neighborhoods were bad. I once taught a course in the Philosophy of Science. In the class, I assigned the reading of an important book by a brilliant philosopher.[22] The class complained that the book was too hard to comprehend and that I should change the book to one it could

---

21 Matthew 18:21–35

22 My course text was Sir Karl R. Popper's *Realism and the Aim of Science* [London: Routledge & Kegan Paul, 1986]

more easily understand. I responded by asking, "Would you rather get an A from understanding an easy book or a B for understanding a book written by one of the finest minds of the twentieth century?" Some in the class got the point. The others either whined or quit. In fact, those who whined did quit, although they stayed in the class.

The point is this. Becoming a disciple of Christ may be one of the hardest things anyone ever undertakes. It requires that those who agree to God's holiness expectations will see the value of the effort in terms of the quality of the outcome. The heart must become pure before the eyes can see God. God is not like some teacher who, for the sake of being pals with his/her students, gives them only what they want. The really good teacher expects the best of his/her students. Those who want to see God without a pure heart will be like the student who wants a college degree by taking the easy courses from easy teachers. These students will never get much clarity, wisdom, or competence. Such a degree is like a pair of reading glasses; it will never compensate for the severe myopia. I could not make a student in any class try to get as much from it as he could. The student must decide that first. This is especially true in moral or holiness matters. One must commit to holiness of the heart before she/he can even see God. Morality or holiness, purity of heart, consists in having the character to live by the four just holiness expectations.

"THE PEACEMAKERS, THOSE WHO ARE PERSECUTED BECAUSE OF RIGHTEOUSNESS, THOSE WHO ARE PERSECUTED FOR THE SAKE OF RIGHTEOUSNESS"

"THOSE WHO ARE INSULTED, PERSECUTED, AND FALSELY ACCUSED OF ALL KINDS OF EVIL BECAUSE OF ME. REJOICE AND BE GLAD BECAUSE GREAT IS YOUR REWARD IN HEAVEN, FOR IN THE SAME WAY THEY PERSECUTED THE PROPHETS WHO WERE BEFORE YOU."

He who would save a drowning person risks harm from the person she/he strives to rescue. This is the plight of the peacemaker. I was once teaching a class on the *Sermon* when we came to this section of the beatitudes. Someone said that our lives become easier when we become peacemakers. People respect peacemakers, it was said, whereupon I asked why it was that they crucified the Prince of Peace.

The peace we are called upon to make is predicated on holiness, but those who want no peace will fight us every inch of the way. There is no room in them for reconciliation, only revenge and reprisal. Yet we are not, as disciples, freed from the responsibility for making peace based on holiness. Gibbon in his *Decline and Fall of the Roman Empire* observed that Rome, when it undertook to persecute Christians, persecuted the best of its citizens. Those who loved peace most were the most vilified. Peter argues in his first epistle that we Christians should not be surprised at the persecution we receive at the hands of the world. If Jesus was murdered for His ministry of truth, righteousness, and goodness, we can expect to be treated no differently.

I regularly teach an undergraduate ethics course. We discover that nearly every theory of ethics tries to define the Good in terms of some form of pleasure or happiness. These theories fail, and yet for as long as ethical thinking has been going on, few philosophers consider that the presumption that morality can be reduced to some notion of pleasure or happiness is wrong headed. Many times, what is moral is not the most pleasurable or creates the most happiness. The most moral, the purest of heart, invites reprisal for exposing the shallowness of seeking happiness. It takes real moral courage to act as a peacemaker when people want no peace based on holiness. Even the best peacemaker cannot make peace between those who persist in hating each other. But we are not let off from this responsibility for this fact. This much the prophets had already understood. *Being the sons of God means being like the Son of God, the Prince of Peace, even if it means being persecuted for righteousness' sake.*

One final note about the term "blessed." Some translations use the term "happy" instead of "blessed." This is perhaps a mistake because it suggests that the purpose in life is to realize happiness or pleasure. Ethics has erred about this for multiple millennia. The first point to make is that the extent to which happiness is a purpose in life is the extent to which we will be seduced into believing that suffering has no place at all. But moral courage, or the courage to become as holy as God expects, faces discomfort, suffering, and in some cases death rather than pursuing happiness or pleasure. For the sake of the pursuit of happiness, many or most will be tempted to forsake moral courage. What appears to be a blessing then becomes a great evil.

There is a great irony in Jesus's words. Blessedness is not the *purpose* of life or living. Righteousness is. Rather, "blessing" is the *result* of living righteously. It is not what the disciple should primarily strive for but what she/he ultimately receives in becoming as holy as God expects. Blessing is the *result* of life dedicated to righteousness, not the *purpose* of life.

After a performance of his *Messiah*, a prominent woman approached Handel and said, "Mr. Handel, I very much enjoyed your performance." Handel responded, "Madam, my purpose was not to entertain you, but to make you better." Thank God there are some people who understand the Kingdom of God! Would that disciples choose God's Kingdom and its values. Jesus's purpose is to make people better. Kingdom disciples choose these values and embark on this process whether their lives go well or ill. And this is only the introduction to the *Sermon*.

CHAPTER 3—THE "GO" PRINCIPLE: MATTHEW 5:13–14

The advertisement for the job says, "Must be a self-starter." Everyone is looking for employees who are "proactive." Proactive people get more done than passive people do. People who sit around and wait for opportunity to knock will wait a long time. Think about this fact compared to the way most people are religious. Most people consider proactive religious people to be nuts or extremists or "zealots." This raises the legitimate question, "Why is there a difference?" Why is it a good quality to be a self-starter in business or career and a bad quality to be so in religion? Why is it a good thing for someone to never take no for an answer in being an effective salesperson or negotiator, while it is "pushy" for a religious person to be so?

The answer must be that it is more important to sell a product line, a service, or a political idea than it is to sell a moral or religious ideal. This is the present state of religious and moral discourse. Everyone is told from primary school through university that personal beliefs are sacred and are immune from criticism or analysis. Personal beliefs are whatever anyone chooses to believe. One must always be sensitive to another's personal beliefs. A person's beliefs are *true for him/her.* It is "inappropriate" for anyone to question whether any personal belief is true. As long as someone believes that something is *true for him/her* and that is that.

There is a failure to recognize that there is an important difference between "what is true *for someone*" and "what is true." Nothing is true simply because someone believes it to be true, no matter how passionately she/he may believe it. However, the only place where people are permitted to hold whatever beliefs they wish is in the arena of ethics and religion. It does not hold for engineers, scientists, accountants, surgeons, and other medical personnel or for airline captains and air-traffic controllers, etc. These people are expected to follow reality, not mere personal belief. The airline captain is not allowed to *feel* that he can make it through the thunderstorm, yet in ethics and religion, how one *feels* is more important than how things are.

THIS PRESENT DARKNESS—MORAL RELATIVITY

Moral relativity is the doctrine that truth and ethics are neither universal nor objective. They are personal and subjective. Truth and Morality are reduced to mere personal beliefs. According to moral relativity, it is improper for anyone to impose a personal truth or personal morality on anyone else. Facts are objective and universal; moral and religious beliefs are subjective and situational. Moral and religious beliefs are values, and values are merely personal. They are subjective. They are just the way people *feel* about things. Facts and values are fundamentally different. They must always be held separate and must never be confused with each other. Facts are the *same* for everyone. Values are *different* for everyone. Facts are *public*; values are *private*.[23]

There is another consequence of this moral relativity. Morality changes. What people may have agreed was morally appropriate or inappropriate at one time or in one place may change. We have all heard someone say "This is the 21st century" in an attempt to justify some action people want to *feel* free to engage in now but was considered immoral in the past. Since morality is nothing more than how people individually *feel* about matters of value, the way one discovers what is moral *for the moment* is to survey the *feelings* of the population.[24] Listen carefully to talk shows or newscasts and documentaries, or take courses in journalism and sociology, and you will notice that the questions are not about what someone thinks but about how someone *feels* about something. The follow-up commentary is based on a statistical analysis assuring us that most of our fellow citizens *feel* that something is or is not okay. It becomes important for people to listen to these reports regularly so they can adjust their personal beliefs to keep pace

---

23 See: David Hume *Treatise on Human Nature* as well as his *Enquiry into the Principles of Morals*.

24 This is based on the descriptivist ethical theory called "Emotivism." It is the view that value statements or value judgments are *nothing more* than articulations of a person's emotional reaction to some event or action.

with the fluidity of current moral trends. It is as though someone says, "Yes, I know that this was considered immoral in the past, but if you survey people now, you'll discover that they no longer *feel* that it is immoral, and so it has become morally permissible." This is a version of the criticism "You're just a prude."

As a result of this silliness, we are in a values crisis. Relativists argue, for example, that women have the right to decide whether babies live or die, but no one has the right to kill an endangered species. My daughter once took a university class titled "Contemporary Religious Ethics." This class was taught in a university with religious origins. An atheist professor taught it. The course addressed no religious ethical framework of any major world religion. (You should have enough information here to explain why this class was not interested in what any religious ethical position was.) In fact, the class should have more accurately carried the title "Contemporary Secular Ethics." The course discussed the ethics of abortion, euthanasia, animal rights, and free expression among other current issues. My daughter, along with her classmates, was told that one *must* be pro-choice in human birth and death, but that no animal *should* be killed. She was told that it was human hubris to place human beings on a higher plane than animals. Animals are members of the same moral community, as are all other species. People who believe that human beings have a privileged moral status are "speciesists" (just as people who believe that one race is superior to another are "racists").[25] Then my daughter asked the professor if he was wearing a leather belt and leather shoes. He was, of course; he said that they were gifts. This class is a microcosm of the state of our world. What was true in this class is true in our culture. Religious beliefs and moral arguments are merely personal and should never be discussed in polite company, and certainly never in an academic setting. Apparently, the only people who can be wrong in their personal beliefs are those who believe that there is objective and universal truth, righteousness, and goodness.

Notice how people who say that *all* moral and religious beliefs are personal and immune from any legitimate criticism are prepared to criticize people who choose a different belief system or values framework. If what they say is true, then I should be able to formulate whatever moral/value belief system I choose. If I should choose to adopt a moral/value system that

---

25 This position is taken by Peter Singer, professor of bio-medical ethics at Princeton University. Carl Sagan, the popularizer of atheist scientism, has also used the term.

says that certain beliefs are wrong and that it is my responsibility to convince people of their error, according to the principle that no one is permitted to question or criticize another's personal beliefs, these people must allow me to do so and never criticize or ridicule my beliefs whatever they may be. A failure to allow me to do so means that the REAL belief is that some personal beliefs are wrong and ought to be exposed and eliminated. But we have already been told that no personal religious or moral belief is right or wrong. It is just whatever it is. Are you not confused by these flip-flops? Which is it? Are personal religious and moral beliefs immune from criticism, or are some true and others false? Both of these positions cannot be true.

METAPHORS OF PRESERVATION AND PENETRATION

After having disclosed the process of becoming a disciple in the beatitudes, Jesus illustrates the consequence of having such disciples in the world. In these metaphors, Jesus provides both a description of how disciples will affect the world and a prescription for how they should affect it. The "is" and the "ought" come together in the life of the disciple of the Kingdom.

> *"You are the salt of the earth. But if the salt loses its saltiness, how can it be made salty again? It is no longer good for anything, except to be thrown out and trampled by men."*

Jesus wonders of what value is a merely personal belief, especially a personal moral belief. There are most certainly personal beliefs that are immune from criticism and are publicly unimportant. Philosophers have long distinguished what is moral from what is immoral and what is nonmoral. Examples of nonmoral things are choices in food, styles in clothing, or preferences in music. One can choose various ways to landscape one's home and not be worried about whether it was moral or immoral. Arranging the furniture, choosing a brand or color of a car, or even the choice of a career all have little to do with moral matters. In general, *nonmoral matters have to do with exercising one's freedom to choose when those choices do not demean the dignity of any person.* The minute one's choices begin to affect the dignity of another is the moment the choices have moral consequences. *So sin is any action or attitude that demeans the dignity of God or any other person.*

Not all personal beliefs or values are nonmoral. Some beliefs, interpersonal or public, have an objective moral quality. Jesus says that the disciple of the Kingdom of Heaven is responsible for being an advocate for what is objectively true, right, and good. It is a foregone conclusion that many people or even most people strive to acquire all of the property, pleasure, power, and prestige as possible, even at the expense of the dignity of oneself or others. Most people have adopted the life principle: "You're first, *after me.*" Only a little reflection exposes the objective consequences of this values orientation. It sets up a system of exploitation that results in the alienation of people from each other as well as considerable interpersonal as well as personal inner conflict.

Jesus accepts none of this. He expects those who would become disciples of the Kingdom to become proactive in addressing, even confronting, people or institutions that advocate or tolerate "You're first, *after me.*" It is not an act of love to allow people to persist in advocating or perpetrating immorality. It is an act of immorality to allow immorality to succeed without facing it. Being the salt of the earth means advocating the moral standard of holiness in a world that wants nothing to do with holiness.

The extent to which a disciple may try to adopt a sort of "Christian relativism" is the extent to which such a disciple makes an unacceptable accommodation to moral indifference. Yet this is exactly the unintended position taken by church leaders and followers. Consider this. Christianity was born into a world of moral decadence and religious paganism. What made the religions pagan was the fact that they tolerated—and in some cases advocated—abjectly immoral behavior and character. Jesus commissions His disciples to "Go and make disciples of all the nations."[26] The first-century disciples obeyed that prime directive, and in about two hundred years, the Twelve transformed the culture of pagan Rome into a Christian culture. What did the early church do differently than it is doing now? Of this, no one can be uncertain. One does not by being passive wrest control from another who is willing to use any and all means to keep its control. The earliest disciples understood that they had to penetrate and transform the culture in which they lived. This means that they had to become proactive. The holiness standards they used to effect this transformation were those God established and Jesus articulated in His ministry.

How is it that we Christians have allowed paganism to retake the culture in less than one hundred years? The answer is that the church has become passive to the world. This became clear to me one evening in a Bible

---

26 Matthew 28:19

study. Someone said, "I keep asking my friend at work to *come to church* and he says he will, but he never does." As clearly as anything I have ever seen, I saw that the commission of Christ had been illicitly altered from "*Go to the world*" to "Invite the world to *come* to church." This is not salting the earth! There is something quite silly about trying to stuff food into a saltshaker. This is the modern "*Come*" paradigm for church. We build "*come to church*" edifices to Christ. One church I know of spent $77 million to serve fourteen thousand people a week. Do the math and discover the cost per attendee (not cost per disciple), and this is only the capital cost. Now add in the interest and operational costs per attendee. *Are there no CPAs and/or MBAs on any church boards?* Is not such a cost a bit too high, compared to the adjusted cost per disciple of the first-century church? But ask a "*Go*" paradigm question: "What kind of ministry to the sick and hungry and thirsty and imprisoned and poor[27] could $77 million plus interest and operational costs buy?"

Consider another case. It makes sense in a "*Come*" paradigm to purchase $250,000 worth of *performance-enhancing* equipment for "praise and worship." But in a "*Go*" paradigm, such budgeting is inconsistent with the prime directive of Christ to make disciples of the nations. When a ministry-enhancing budget affecting the lives of the disenfranchised and forgotten barely breaks into four figures and certainly rarely reaches five figures, this is salt-less-ness. *Preaching comforting sermons and giving "uplifting" performances to the converted is salt without saltiness.* The best choirs in the world singing glorious praises to God does not compensate for ignoring those whom God loves just as much as He loves those in the audiences of Branson- or Las Vegas–style concerts. It is a bit like having a Father's Day celebration for a father, but only those of the family can come who sing and play the best. The rest of the family is left out. I would not tolerate this of my family, nor would I suspect that God would. If the justification were that we could not send invitations to some of our brothers and sisters because we had to make sure we had enough to pay for the banquet hall and sound equipment, I would be furious. Does anybody think that God would be any less so? Does anyone want to presume to argue for very long that He would not be so? *This is salt without saltiness.*

> *"You are the light of the world. A city set on a hill cannot be hidden. Neither do people light a lamp and put it under a*

---

27 Matthew 25:31–46

bowl. Instead they put it on its stand, and it gives light to the whole house. In the same way let your light shine before men, that they may see your good works and glorify your Father who is in Heaven."

If building temples to ourselves is salt without saltiness, what is salt that is salty? Just think about the difference between *"Go"* and *"Come."* Jesus's ministry was one of going to where people are. He went from city to city and village to village. He went to and was criticized for associating with the *"hoi polloi,"* with prostitutes and tax-collecting extortionists. I have to tell you one of many stories about how the battle against the *"come"* paradigm goes. A woman and her family started coming to our church. I call her "the spandex lady" because she wore spandex shorts and a tank top to services. The family would invariably come late and walk right down the middle aisle. The father had not yet discovered the point of the shower stall. The two children gave new meaning to the notion "snot-nosed." As you might guess, they were out of place in our middle-class, quasi-professional church. At first, the giggles were discretely suppressed. The longer this family came and tried to be a part of the body, the less discrete the sniggering became. One day when I visited the spandex lady, she said to me, "I'm not going to let those people run us off!" She was wrong. They did, for no one can take rudeness and demeaning indefinitely. The tragedy of this story is that one group of Christians ran off another. *As absolutely blasphemous as this is, it is even more so for Christians who have tasted the heavenly gift to refuse to take it to the "spandex families" that do not come to church.*

In another sermon, Jesus describes His mission to His hometown synagogue. He begins with a quotation from Isaiah: "The spirit of the Lord is upon me to peach good news to the poor, release to the captives, and sight to the blind."[28] Those present thought well of Him until they heard the sermon. He said that among all of the widows in Israel, a prophet of Israel ministered to none but a Gentile widow of Sidon.[29] Further, among all of the many lepers in Israel, a prophet of Israel ministered to none but a Gentile military commander of Syria.[30] The point of the message was obvious to all present. *God's love extends beyond the provincial vision of the*

---

28   Luke 4:18

29   I Kings 17:9

30   II Kings 5:14

chauvinistic. The Jewish nation was to have been a light to the nations, yet their light was placed delicately under quite luxurious peck measures. The Temple was wonderfully splendid. Synagogues were too. Yet their message was for only those people who were most like them. The point of Jesus's sermon was singularly unambiguous, and for being so audacious in proclaiming it, He was attacked and, but for His personal magnanimity, would have been killed.

It is a fact that people with a holiness core will enlighten the places where they live. When people behave morally, articulate moral values, and argue for moral character, the light from their presence will always have to be dealt with. I was invited by my church to participate on a strategic planning committee. The purpose of the committee was to develop a plan for the growth of our church. I suspected that the operative term in this phrase was "our." But I thought that there was an outside chance that the "our" could be replaced with the more proper term "Christ's." I argued that spending several million dollars on a "come facility" was inconsistent with the "go directive." I recommended that we take about half of the money and buy one of many abandoned houses in critical neighborhoods in our town. We could buy them quite inexpensively, and the skill to renovate them was free since people in the church could do the work. We have, after all, carpenters, engineers, architects, contractors, electricians, plumbers, etc., in the congregation. We could convert these buildings into several neighborhood ministry centers. The social workers, attorneys, teachers, and teacher's aides could staff these centers as professional volunteers. We could get a nearby seminary to provide interns in counseling to assist with the myriad of problems people have in addiction recovery, domestic relations, and child rearing. The objection raised against this proposal was that "people were already too busy" and our attendance at church services and church functions would suffer. The die was cast. Once it becomes more important to support programs for *our* members than programs for people who live in misery and despair and in need of Christ, I knew it was all over. My parting mention was that the churches of the Revelation were, save for one, called upon to repent or else lose their lampstands. No one had the ears to hear.

It does not stop here. I was in a staff planning meeting once when, while we were on a break for lunch, the minister of music (more properly the minister of singing and dancing) said that she was going to have to fire her praise band drummer. When we asked why such a drastic action was called for (surely he must have been engaged in something outrageously immoral), she said that he just couldn't keep time well enough. Later, when I was asked for the issues in my area, I started by saying that we could equip people in adult education for being more effective witnesses in the workplace if we set standards for our adult teachers. Asked how I would do such a thing, I recommended that we test people who would become teachers. If they failed to show sufficient competence, then we would take them out of the classroom and put them into a series of courses to address the competency lag. My colleagues were aghast. We could do no such thing, for then we would have no teachers at all. I then asked why it was okay to "fire" a drummer who has only a performance role but not okay to set and enforce excellence standards for adult Sunday school teachers when they had an equipping role. There was no answer, but plenty of anger. All was very clear. Elevating the standards of excellence for students and teachers was intolerable because people would stop *coming*, but perfectly appropriate for those whose ministries keep people *coming* to church services.

Jesus's teaching can hardly be clearer. Build the cities on the hilltops and place the lights on the lampstands. It makes no sense at all to turn on a flashlight and then return it into a drawer. The batteries don't last long enough the way it is without leaving them on wastefully. Jesus *goes* to the sinner. Had He waited for them to *come* to Him, the church would still be in Jerusalem—if it had survived at all.

CHAPTER 4—THE SURPASSING RIGHTEOUSNESS: MATTHEW 5:15–20

When the potential for confusion exists in presenting a new message, one must make clear in the beginning what one does not mean. Jesus is no different. The Jewish religion relied on Law, and so did the administration of the Roman Empire. To be sure, Jewish Law was based on the Law of God, notwithstanding the rabbinic distortions of it. But Law carries with it a certain inherent inadequacy. Jesus will take us to a new level—a level that is compatible with Law, but is superior to Law. Anyone who would become a citizen of God's Kingdom must surpass legalism, i.e., using the Law to specify what people are required to do or are prohibited from doing. In appreciating this insufficiency, Aristotle remarked that "the righteous man needs no law."[31] To understand this remark is to understand what Jesus means by saying, "Unless your righteousness surpasses that of the scribes and Pharisees, you will by no means enter the Kingdom of Heaven." [32]

This statement is the thesis of the *Sermon on the Mount*. The rest of the *Sermon* is nothing more than an explanation of this thesis. For those of us who want to participate in God's Kingdom, comprehending its meaning becomes the most important thing in life. Let's see whether we can comprehend it.

Jesus first comments that people will be tempted to construe His *Sermon* as an abrogation of law, that Jesus advocates the irrelevance of Law. Since the Pharisees and scribes teach and practice the primacy of Law, Jesus's concern for being misunderstood is well placed. Jesus makes clear that He

---

31   See: Aristotle's *Nichomachean Ethics*

32   Matthew 5:20

will tolerate no lawlessness at all. Antinomianism[33] is far from His meaning. *He advocates not the abolition of law, but its fulfillment.* He wants to make this abundantly clear. It is also clear that people who use the law to exploit and demean others will not participate in the Kingdom. Jesus rejects both legalism and antinomianism. So the question is "what surpasses something that is necessary?"

THE STRATEGY OF OPAQUENESS

There is a significant moral difference between "doing good" and "being good." It is quite easy to see that one can "do good things" without "being good." Consider this. Someone whose character is good will consistently "do good," while those whose character is compromised can and do use "doing good" to perpetrate malice or deception. In this case, "doing good" is opaque so as to hide the thoughts and intentions of the heart. One cannot very well perpetrate malice and deception by being transparent, for if thoughts, intentions, and strategies were transparently portrayed, none but the hopelessly naive would be deceived. This is the point of the Oscar Wilde novel and motion picture *The Picture of Dorian Gray.* A quite handsome man had a portrait made of himself in his youth. He wished that he would always remain as handsome as the picture portrayed him. The picture would show the real Dorian as he aged. As Dorian lived a life of deception, manipulation, exploitation, greed, and lust, the picture changed to reveal the ugliness of this man's life while his body retained its beauty. In the end, Dorian went to see the portrait and died at its ugliness.

Appearances are generally quite deceiving. The inadequacy of legalism lies in its presumption that appearances are reality, that complying with the law behaviorally makes one righteous. Believing that "behaving rightly" means the same thing as "being righteous" is a serious mistake in moral reasoning. There can be no room for this mistake in the Kingdom disciple. A God who is duped by this ruse or would decide on issues of holiness in this way would hardly be worthy of worship and certainly would not be just. Nor will any of us who are not hopelessly naïve be so duped. It would be quite remarkable for Jesus to fail to take into account the strategy of opaqueness for deceiving and manipulating others.

---

33 Antinomianism is the belief that no law is necessary because individual freedom is primary.

No one can consistently "do good" without "being good." But it is possible from time to time. The clever elevate this skill of deception. It is also possible for someone to "be good" while sometimes "not doing good." Although one might think this is too much ambiguity, there is an important difference. The deeds of a person whose character is good are more transparent than someone whose deeds are opaque with regard to his/her character. In other words, *one can better infer immoral character from immoral actions than to infer good character from good actions.*

In the movie *Gandhi,* there is a scene in which Gandhi expected his wife, like everyone else, to rake and cover the latrine. Everyone was to be regarded as equal in the ashram. She refused to do this work because it was, in her value system, the work of untouchables. Gandhi begins to exercise his legal right to divorce her and banish her from his home and the ashram. She protests by demanding, "Have you no shame?" Gandhi catches himself and slumps into a chair, asking, "What is the matter with me?" She responds by saying, "You're human, and *most of us don't even want to be as good as you do.*"[34] Gandhi's wife discovers what God looks for in people. He wants people to want to be good. For those who want to "be good" there can be neither the deception of oneself nor of others. God wants people who want to be as good as possible. The good person and the bad one both may do good deeds. But the good person rarely does bad ones, and when it does occur, no one is more distraught. It is rare, even difficult, for someone who wants to become holy in character to act immorally.

RANKING MORAL ACTIONS

When I teach my ethics course to prison inmates, I make sure we always discuss the moral ranking of certain moral situations. One of my favorite questions is to ask which of two alternatives is the most moral. Who acts with a higher order morality: someone who does what is moral to gain some reward or to avoid some punishment, or a person who does what is moral independently of any reward or punishment? This type of question establishes the same moral action with different moral motivations. The answer is consistent: "Doing good" without a consideration of reward or punishment is the higher order morality. Someone who wants to be so good

---

34 John Briley, Gandhi, http://www.gandhiserve.org/video/gandhi_screenplay.html 1982, pg 30.

that the consequences of "doing good" (whether rewards or punishments) are irrelevant have a righteousness that surpasses that of the scribes and Pharisees. When one can see this, one understands another dimension of what Jesus means by a "surpassing righteousness."

The ability to rank moral alternatives reveals something very important. It reveals that people have the necessary knowledge of moral principles. It reveals that this knowledge is virtually universal. This knowledge exists prior to the presence of Law. It has a logical as well as moral priority. My experience in teaching prison inmates makes this result even more impressive. A good act or behavior without a good character is not righteous at all. It is deception or hypocrisy, but it certainly is not righteous.

MORAL ACTIONS, MORAL CHARACTER AND MORAL WORTH

Generally, the reason most people give for not acting in a moral way is that to do so is to act against some natural instinct or appetite. It has become a conventional wisdom within moral relativism to say that one can never be held morally responsible for acting according to a natural instinct or appetite. Indeed, it is foolhardy to expect people to act contrary to natural instincts or appetites.[35] Given a circumstance that requires people to expose themselves to danger most will try various strategies to justify not endangering themselves. "I would act to save a family member or friend, but this is a stranger" or "my family needs me" or "both of us will be harmed to no effect."

To expose the devastating effect of this reasoning, the philosopher Immanuel Kant argued that no action has moral worth unless the action is done *against* one's inclinations to so act.[36] An act of moral courage consists in acting according to one's moral duty even when one's natural appetites and instincts incline him/her to do otherwise. For this, Kant argues, one must have a Good Will to exercise control over the appetites and instincts. On the surface, this seems a very good standard for evaluating someone's character. It is clearly superior to the reasoning of Thomas Hobbes[37] and

---

35 We owe this reasoning primarily to Thomas Hobbes's *Leviathan* and David Hume's *Treatise on Human Nature* as well as his *An Enquiry Concerning Human Understanding.*

36 *The Fundamental Principles of the Metaphysic of Morals* 1785

37 *Leviathan* 1651

David Hume.[38] Those who give priority to instinct must justify someone's not acting with moral courage. There would be neither moral courage nor moral cowardice. Kant disagrees with such a conclusion. For example, the *instinct* for self-preservation constitutes an inclination *not* to act in some dangerous situation. When someone's life is in danger, there is a *principle of moral duty* that compels one to endanger her/himself in order to save the life of another. According to Kant, the act of a person to save the life of another in some dangerous circumstance is an act of moral courage, of moral worth, since such a person acts against the *inclination* to preserve him/herself.

There is something intuitively correct in Kant's notion of moral worth. One must often override one's appetitive inclinations in order to do one's moral duty. But we are at once faced with an entirely unacceptable moral conclusion by applying Kant's moral worth standard. What is the moral worth of the action of a policeman or fireman or paramedic or soldier or even a parent for that matter? Presumably, since these people have been trained to suppress their fears, and so they act according to their inclinations to act bravely and decisively, their actions are no longer morally worthwhile. My ethics students pick up on this right away. Both classes of people are acting with moral worth. One could argue, quite compellingly, that some *acts* of moral courage are indeed based in moral cowardice since some people will do something good because they are afraid of being ostracized for their cowardice should they fail to do so. This seems right. So the question arises, "In what do acts of moral worth or moral courage consist?" The answer lies in the moral character of a person, i.e., "being good" once again is more morally significant than merely "doing good." Indeed, Kant calls this the "Good Will."

Now, consider this. *What is the moral status of an action that is compelled by law?* What if one acts to save a life or do some good for someone at the same time that some law compels one to act to save a life or do some good? Will such an action be good? Will a person who complies with such a law be good? It should be clear that *the introduction of laws cheapens actions of moral worth.* Therefore, Law is secondary to morality.

Laws are necessary to govern people whose moral character is in some sense deviant. Laws are unnecessary for people whose character is formed to "be good." For example, several years ago in a Las Vegas casino, a young adult male lured a preteen girl into a men's restroom. There he

38 *An Enquiry Concerning the Principles of Morals* 1751

repeatedly sodomized her while his "buddy" watched, left, and returned to watch some more. When the authorities investigated, they arrested the two men. A while later, the perpetrator was indicted and his "buddy" was released. As one might imagine, there was a swell of moral outrage that this "nonparticipating" man was not charged. The district attorney held a news conference to explain that there was no statute under which this man could be charged. What he did or, more precisely, did not do, was "not illegal." *It was clearly immoral, but it was "not illegal."*

Now that there is a law under which such people can be charged, the act of a person of moral character and courage is cheapened since now there is no overt way of knowing whether someone acts on moral principle or merely out of legal obligation. Clearly, someone who does something right or good because there is a law compelling him/her to do so has done something less morally worthwhile than someone who would comply with the morality behind the law even if no law existed. In this Las Vegas case, apparently no one had ever considered that anyone would ever act as this second man did. There is no need for a law to cover immoral things that no one would ever think of doing. It becomes necessary for a new law to be enacted once someone sinks to some new level of depravity. The implementation of law lags behind the perpetration of immorality. *Laws are for the lawless—not for those of moral character, not for the righteous.*

Soren Kierkegaard improved on Kant's view.[39] Kierkegaard asked whether or not a person was moral in virtue of a moral act that had moral worth merely because someone complied with a moral standard of duty or obligation. His answer was that it was not. What is necessary is *not* that one complies with one's moral duty due to an external principle of moral obligation. What is necessary is that the moral principle is internalized in a person's character. When someone has moral character, she/he no longer needs an external law or moral standard. So it is easy to see what Aristotle meant by the comment that "The righteous man needs no law." I have no doubt that this is also what Jesus means. A righteousness that fails to surpass the law-based expectations of the scribes and Pharisees is wholly inadequate in characterizing the righteousness of a Kingdom disciple. Even when the Law is perfect and good, as the Law of God is, it is not sufficient for someone to comply with it as an external standard of right and wrong.

---

39 See Kierkegaard's *Either/Or* as well as his *On Fear and Trembling* and *Stages Along Life's Way.*

The Kingdom disciple must base his/her compliance on the requisite moral character. Complying with the Law, even the Law of God, is necessary but not sufficient for qualifying as a Kingdom disciple. What is both necessary and sufficient is compliance with moral duty first in character and then in actions.

To illustrate this principle, I ask my Sunday school classes to consider the fact that most of the laws of our society are completely irrelevant to most people in the room. The State of Illinois needs no law against murder or extortion or rape or perjury or stealing to keep me/us from doing these things. I need no law to force me to drive responsibly. My children need no law to protect them from my abusing them. In general, the Kingdom disciple needs few of the laws any State finds that it must pass. This is a consistent principle of Christian conduct in the Bible. Paul says in Romans that no Christian needs to be threatened by the power of the State to punish people, since Christians will already comply with the moral law from their hearts.[40] Peter says in his first epistle that if Christians should have to suffer at the hands of the Law, then let it be because the Law is unjust, not because Christians are.[41]

The holiness standard has just become elevated. No longer is it sufficient to merely comply with some law in order to be moral; one has to comply with what is moral even if there were no law. So one needs to have a prior understanding of what is holy because when there is no law to guide someone in acting with holiness or in developing a holy character, the law cannot be the standard of what is true, right, and good. The increasing number of laws required for a society is proportional to the increase in the immoral character of its population. The more laws are necessary to prescribe what people should do or proscribe what they should not do, the more it is evident that people have immoral proclivities. Conversely, the more a society is comprised of people with moral character, the fewer laws it needs.

> *"Do not begin to think that I have come to abrogate the Law or the prophets. I have not come to abrogate them but to fulfill them . . . Unless your righteousness surpasses that of the scribes and Pharisees, you shall by no means enter the Kingdom of Heaven."*

---

40 See: Romans 13:1 ff.

41 See: I Peter 2

CHAPTER 5—Beyond the Conventional Wisdom: Matthew 5:21–48

Recall the four Kingdom values of chapter 1. We can constantly compare them with what Jesus says in the *Sermon*. Jesus either specifically advocates them, or He presupposes them. Look for them in your study of the rest of the *Sermon*. Here they are again:

1. Every person is morally responsible for treating *all* people with dignity and respect, since God has created *all* people in His image.
2. Every person is morally responsible for moral goodness in himself and others.
3. Every person is morally responsible for being an advocate for what is true, right, and good.
4. Every person is morally responsible for being proactive in the reconciliation of *all* people to God and to each other.

Furthermore, recall the thesis of the *Sermon*. For anyone to enter God's Kingdom, it is necessary to "surpass the righteousness of the scribes and Pharisees." In fact, Jesus uses one of the strongest possible Koine Greek negatives when He says, "you will *by no means* enter . . ."[42] If you want to enter God's Kingdom, as I do, it becomes imperative to comprehend what this means and to comply with its demands.

Jesus illustrates how the "surpassing righteousness" goes well beyond the conventional wisdom. Conventional wisdom centers on *acceptable* arguments for compromising holiness. When an argument justifies some departure

---

42 Matthew 5:20 [οὐ μὴ εἰσέλθητε εἰς τὴν βασιλείαν τῶν οὐρανῶν.]

from holiness, there is a logic of compromise. It is a deceptive practice. It justifies deviations from the four Kingdom values. The conventional wisdom dumbs down God's standard of holiness. It compromises God's just holiness expectations. Jesus sets a higher moral standard. It surpasses the moral expectations of the teachers of the conventional wisdom.

A Higher Moral Logic

Jesus brilliantly begins by formulating a higher moral logic than His predecessors use. The conventional wisdom uses the logic of exceptions, the logic of justifications. For any moral principle, there is always a lurking exception. In my World Religions classes, we discover that the holiness expectations of nearly all religions agree on the basic moral universals. We call this "moral homogeneity." The question we face is how it is that such moral homogeneity exists. The straightforward explanation was that they are, to borrow from computer jargon, "hardwired" into us as human beings. God created people with these moral principles just as He created them with the principles of mathematics or logic. God created the universe such that it interfaces with these moral universals as He created the universe to interface with our knowledge of mathematics and logic. Einstein said he believed in God precisely because there is mathematics and logic. The structure of the universe itself interfaces with the math and logic in the mind of man. Perhaps we can add that we can believe in God because of moral homogeneity too.

This answer goes against the grain of moral relativists. They argue that the more important fact is the diversity of moral standards between cultures. There can be no moral universals in people because there is no God. There is only natural evolution. For example, Frederick Nietzsche argues that moral standards are merely those that the powerful impose on the weaker.[43] So there can be moral universals only when there is a universal might. The problem for relativists is that if evolution satisfactorily explains morality, it must also explain how mathematics and logic are also relative to where we are in our evolution. Admittedly, there are important differences in moral principles between cultures. But why should this diversity cover up the obvious homogeneity? Further, why should we be blind to the fact that acceptable

---

43 Consider other philosophers with a similar thesis, as, for example: Thomas Hobbes, Charles Darwin, Sigmund Feud and Karl Marx.

morality in some cultures is plainly immoral? The Nazi policy of genocide is not morally appropriate even though it was culturally acceptable.

Moral relativity reduces to "might makes right." The logic of justification permits people to justify a departure from the moral high ground when some perceived immorality has demeaned them or theirs. During the Clinton administration, there was a quasi-war fought in the Balkans between ethnic peoples. The Serbs held political and military control over the Kosovar Albanians. The Serbs initiated a policy of ethnic cleansing. Ultimately, this policy was called in question on the basis that politics and power never justify the violations human of rights. When the Serbs refused to modify their policy, NATO initiated air strikes to diminish the capacity of the Serbs to carry out their policy of genocide. What was interesting were the arguments the Serbs and Serb sympathizers used to justify Serb policy. First, there was the justification based on the historical fact that the Albanians once persecuted the Serbs ["An eye for an eye"]. Second, the Serbs were justified because the Kosovar Albanians were Nazi sympathizers ["Hate your enemy"]. The strategies justified lying in treaties and in propaganda ["Let your 'yes' be 'yes' and your 'no' be 'no'"]. So no one could believe the word of political leaders. After all, one is justified in loving one's neighbors and countrymen, but also justified in hating one's enemies. However, the "war" was won by superior air power, not by moral reasoning. This is due to the fact that *moral reasoning does not compel immoral people.*

There is no reason to restrict this logic to international politics. It operates in every aspect of human endeavor. People may always depart from the higher moral ground when "justified." They merely have to develop an argument of justification. It becomes easier for people to do this when moral universals and moral logic have been emasculated by moral relativism. Far from diminishing conflict, moral relativism intensifies it. When there is no universal moral standard by which one can assess what to do, the only remaining mechanism for resolving conflict is might.

In each of the *Sermon's* five illustrations Jesus presents in the *Sermon*, Jesus elevates the standard of moral conduct. He argues that attempts to use moral justification will always fail to attain to the standard of God's just holiness expectations. Jesus presents us with a logic of the moral high ground. No deviation from God's just holiness expectations is ever morally justified. The four Kingdom values are never compromised. To do so is to sin. The four Kingdom values must be applied in a balanced way. Let's see how Jesus does this.

"EMOTION-BASED" VERSUS "WILL-BASED" MORALITY

No one will disagree that murder is immoral. That is why it is illegal. Something nearly always goes unnoticed in these pairs that contrast the conventional wisdom of the logic of justification with the "But I say to you." In a few short sentences, Jesus's moral logic surpasses the moral logic of justification.

First, notice that Jesus distinguishes between a behavior (i.e., murder) and the trait-control of an emotion (i.e., "self-control" and "anger"). Since the influence of the moral philosophy of Hobbes and Hume, emotions are merely matters of fact having no moral status at all. Emotions, they argued, are natural. They are based in biochemistry. No one can be expected to contravene the operation of such natural laws. No act of the will is sufficient to stop the operation of the hormones and enzymes at work in one's brain. An emotion may be acknowledged, but it cannot be evaluated. An emotion is just whatever it is. Read any textbook in psychology or any self-improvement book and you will discover this logic of man's moral impotence before his brain chemistry. The implication is that once an emotion "kicks in," what one does becomes irresistible. Moral responsibility ends with the beginning of the emotions. All kinds of behaviors are mitigated both in and out of court by referring to some underlying emotional condition that is, in turn, reduced to some psychochemical cause.

By this logic, if there is any remnant of moral responsibility, it lies with the person(s) whose behavior triggers the emotion. "It's not my fault, he made me mad!" This need not be merely interpersonal anger. Anger, in contemporary reasoning, may arise due to institutional or historical causes [slavery or patriarchy] or sociological conditions [ghettos and "glass ceilings"]. "My anger is not my fault. It is due to my alienation because of your exploitative practices." Can you see the justification of "an eye for an eye" in these arguments? Certainly, neither Jesus nor I condone any violation of any of the just holiness principles. The question is whether one is morally justified in using anger to justify counterexploitation. As Gandhi says in the spirit of Christ, "An eye for an eye makes the whole world blind."[44]

Jesus accepts no part of this logic of justification. Jesus expects everyone to have the capacity to exercise self-control in overriding emotions. The

---

44 *Peace: The Words and Inspiration of Mahatma Gandhi* [Boulder, CO: Blue Mountain Press, 2007], pg. 25.

morally superior person, the person of surpassing righteousness, overrides the impulses of the emotions, interrupting any animalistic response to any stimuli whether external or internal. Immanuel Kant criticized Hobbes and Hume by saying that the *Good* person is a person of a *Good* Will. A *Good* Will is a will that invokes moral duty, moral obligation to check animalistic emotion. Jesus had already said this much. The fact that someone is angry is never a moral justification for murder, name-calling, or any other demeaning behavior. The first moral principle is that all people are created in God's image and therefore deserve to be treated with dignity and respect—even if I am angry or someone has made me angry. My anger never justifies my calling anyone by any demeaning epithet, whether "Racca" or "Thou fool" or "You idiot." As my parents justifiably said, "Control your mouth!"

"Negative" versus "Positive" Morality

Self-control goes further than merely restricting the behavioral expressions of anger, for this is a negative morality. Negative morality says, "Don't do something, or control your impulse to do something wrong." Jesus's logic includes "control your impulse" as well as doing something positive. Jesus's positive moral logic surpasses a negative moral logic by prescribing what behaviors to do as well as what traits undergird the behaviors themselves.

The logic of reconciliation is a positive moral logic. Jesus directly applies one of the moral principles above. Every person is responsible for being proactive in the reconciliation of all people to God and to each other. Anger cannot be proactive in this way. Anger sulks and pouts. Anger seethes and resents. And, ultimately, anger lashes out against whatever is at hand, whether there is any justification for it or not. The inferior moral logic explains away the moral responsibility. Jesus's moral logic demands that people transcend their anger in order to initiate reconciliation. People who are angry, whether justified or not, are expected to go to anyone who has something against them. A gift for God on His altar is tainted unless and until the one who offers it initiates reconciliation with the offended brother. It becomes holy when she/he who gives it complies with the fourth just holiness expectation.

"External" versus "Internal" Morality

The surpassing moral motivation is for someone to initiate reconciliation and to do so from having internalized principles of moral obligation as traits of character. Soren Kierkegaard criticized Kant's moral logic because he failed to distinguish between people who do what is right due to some external standard or threat of punishment or prospect of reward and those who do what is right for the sake of righteousness itself. Kierkegaard called the former the "ethical consciousness." This is good as far as it goes, but the surpassing righteousness consists in a person's accepting the moral responsibility for acquiring virtuous moral traits. Kierkegaard argued that it is morally superior for one to pass through the ethical consciousness to what he called the Religious Consciousness.[45] Like Abraham, "the Knight of Faith" is the one who does what is right because she/he has chosen to be a person of virtuous character. A person of *faith* is one who complies with God's holiness expectations from having internalized the principles of holiness in his/her character.

Jesus had already said what Kierkegaard came to teach. Forcing someone to comply with moral standards makes no one sufficiently holy. Only when the holiness standard becomes internalized in character does one comply with the *Sermon's* thesis: "Unless your righteousness surpasses that of the scribes and Pharisees, you will by no means enter the Kingdom of Heaven."[46] It is in choosing to become a "Knight of Faith" that provides a sufficient condition for entry to Heaven's Kingdom, not the *de facto* completion of the process. The one who has chosen to become as holy as God expects is the person who accepts *responsibility* for his/her sins, the one who experiences *remorse* for them, who *repudiates* them and *resolves* to comply with God's just holiness expectations whether his/her life goes well or ill.

Some people need the threat of punishment to motivate them to accept the responsibility for becoming Kierkegaard's "Knight of Faith," so Jesus provides this motivation. But no one needs to labor under any illusion that compliance under the threat of punishment reaches the moral level of the surpassing righteousness. Such a one must get beyond compelling punishments or even beatific rewards in order to qualify as a Kingdom disciple.

---

45   See his: *Fear and Trembling*

46   Matthew 5:20

CHAPTER 6—Beyond the Conventional Wisdom: Adultery and Divorce: Matthew 5:27–32

Jesus addresses one of the most prominent issues of human life and morality: sex. Throughout the Old and New Testament, there is a definite expectation of sexual propriety. Given the current state of permissive sexuality, what are we to make of Jesus's expectation of a "surpassing righteousness" with regard to sex?

The Doctrine of the Total Animality of Man

Sexuality is a natural appetite. It has complex physiological and psychological dimensions. If we were to follow the logic of the conventional wisdom, we would explain the moral aspects of sexuality in terms of these physiological and psychological forces. Once again, we owe our present logic of sexuality to Thomas Hobbes and David Hume. According to them, and those who follow their logic, humans are nothing more than complex animals. This belief is called the *total animality of man* doctrine. Morality is nothing more than following one's natural appetites and aversions. Instincts, urges, and impulses are what they are, and no one can override them. According to these men, when natural appetites occur in people, it is no different than when they occur in animals. When animals experience reproductive instincts, one of two things occurs. Either the urge to mate and reproduce is satisfied, or the animal dies trying.

This animality logic has overtaken sexual ethics in the secular world. The philosophy has been with us for some time, but its effects have become widespread over the past fifty years. Not long ago, the cultural expectation, due to Judeo-Christian influences, was that people would exercise self-control over sexual urges until marriage. Men were to treat women like ladies. [I doubt that women would take lightly to being referred to as animals.] Ladies were to make sure that no man got too familiar in "taking liberties." Women who gave too freely and men who took too freely were never esteemed in their communities. Adultery and divorce occurred in these times, but they were—at least publicly—taken with societal disapproval.

Now the enlightened humanist elite tells us that the premise under which "Judeo-Christian" society enforced these parochial standards of sexual morality is entirely misguided and unfounded. They assure us that their biological studies of *animal behavior* reveal that, due to our so-called evolutionary past, the sexual urge is so strong that to expect people to exercise self-control over such natural urges is silly, misguided, and the cause of many psychological maladies.[47] Consequently, fifty years ago the cultural, educational, religious, and family message was: "Don't engage in sex before marriage and then only with your "till death do us part" spouse. The new so-called enlightened message is: "Sex is natural, and nothing natural is bad. So when you have sex, make sure that it is safe sex." Children need to be sexualized according to this animality logic. Hence schools should teach sex education as early as possible. Since parents are not likely to understand this "enlightened" point of view, the enlightened elite must dispense animality sex education surreptitiously. The theme is: "These are the techniques for enjoying 'safe' sex, and if something happens that a girl or woman becomes pregnant, abortion is morally permissible, even appropriate." After all, unwanted children become burdens to our pleasure and a hindrance to our fulfillment as well as that of others.

Further, according to the enlightened elite, divorce and remarriage are merely stages in life. As people go through their life phases, their needs change, so their marital partners will have to change to satisfy these needs. Consequently, one marital partner gives way to another more suitable one. This is called "serial monogamy." "Serial monogamy" is natural. Therefore, by this logic, divorce is a good thing. Soon, the extension of this logic will justify everything from polygamy and polyandry to swinging and pedophilia. Sexuality, we are assured, is an expression of love, and no expression of love should be restricted either morally or legally. Jealousy restricts love, and so it is bad—a "hang-up" from the "uptight" Judeo-

---

47   As in, for example, Sigmund Freud

Christian past. *There can be no moral injunction against any natural urge.* This is the logic of "enlightened" sexuality.

ARE HUMAN BEINGS NOTHING BUT ANIMALS?

Have you asked the critical question yet? Shall we succumb to the animality argument of the enlightened elite? Here is the fundamental question: Are animal studies sufficient to explain, in principle, *all* human behavior? Why should we, or anyone for that matter, allow that *all* human behavior is sufficiently explained in terms of underlying animal behavior? Perhaps human beings are not *merely* animals. Humans certainly do have *some* of the characteristics of animals. But why should we suppose that humans have *all and only* the characteristics of animals? The burden of proof for this form of scientific reductionism lies with the enlightened elite. Perhaps morality, as well as some other things, cannot be reduced to animal studies because—in some very important respects—human beings are unique in the universe. Perhaps human beings have properties that are absent in animals. Perhaps human beings and animals differ in kind, not in degree.[48]

In the 1961 movie *Spartacus*, promising slaves were taken to gladiator training facilities. They were trained to fight and kill each other in the Roman circus. As a reward for attaining excellence in their training, gladiator trainees were given slave women, often girls, for their sexual gratification. At one point in the movie, the character in the title role is given a beautiful slave girl. Spartacus reflects on this circumstance. Of course, it would be enjoyable to take her sexually, but the moment he does so, he affirms what his owners and trainers believe about him. He becomes a head of livestock. At the point of this reflection, Spartacus screams, not sure that anyone will hear or pay any attention, "I am not an animal!"

Jesus agrees with Spartacus. Men and women are created in God's image and so deserve to be treated with dignity and respect. It would seem that this needs little or no argument. Treat a man or a woman as you would treat an animal, even a pet, and you will have demeaned the dignity of that person. Any person so ill-treated will, sooner rather than later, figure this out too. It is an existential reality as much as a theological or philosophical truth. Most people resent being treated like animals. When people do treat others

---

48 See: Mortimer Adler *The Difference of Man and the Difference it Makes* [New York, NY: World Publishing, 1967]

like animals, there is an instant and intuitive outrage. The Nazis, abusive or neglectful spouses or parents, police officers exercising brutal force in their duties, and yes, assault, rape, and murder are morally outrageous because they fundamentally demean the dignity of a human being. Animals can be used for various purposes [e.g., food, medical experimentation, and clothing] without engendering legitimate moral outrage, PETA and Peter Singer notwithstanding. I can even run over a wild animal or a pet with my car and, as bad as I may feel about it, there is no moral fault. Prison riots[49] have occurred due to the presumption that once someone demeans another human being, she/he no longer deserves humane treatment. Those prison riots scream the same words as Spartacus: "I am not an animal!" This reveals the existential denial of the *total animality of man doctrine.*

As there is an existential reason to object to this doctrine, there is an objective reason as well. People can change and acquire certain traits, namely character traits (i.e., virtues and vices). Conversely, although one can somewhat manage animal behavior, one cannot alter animal traits. It is a stretch to believe or argue that animals can acquire moral character traits (i.e., virtues and vices). Taking the cute little tiger cub as a family pet is a bad idea since its cuteness disappears when the pet becomes an adult and regards the baby as a meal or an adult as a rival. Cage the cat when it is compelled by its instincts to look for a mate and see what happens. Enter the cage to reason morally with the cat and get mauled. No one will ever think that there is any moral fault in the cat. The moral fault lies with people, with the one who stupidly tries to ignore or contravene the cat's natural traits.[50]

But with humans, it is different. No one, not even the most ardent moral relativist, can resist making moral judgments. Aristotle claimed that man is unique in that he is the "rational" animal. Man is rational, and animals are not so in the same qualitative sense. So, it seems, Aristotle could well have designated human beings as the "ethical" animal. Even with this, we must disagree. Humans are ethical, rational creatures—not merely animals.

JESUS AND SEXUAL MORALITY

The conventional wisdom in Jesus's time was that no one was permitted to commit adultery. After all, the Mosaic Law specifically prohibited it.

---

49   Recall the Attica riots in 1971.

50   This is the lesson in H. G. Wells' story *The Island of Dr. Moreau.*

It all seems pretty clear-cut until we apply the logic of justification. What are the circumstances under which adultery can exist? As the forty-second president says, "I did not have 'sexual relations' *as I understand the meaning of that term.*" The logic of justification looks for the ambiguities in the law and then seeks to exploit them for one's permissive advantage. If the Law is not written clearly enough, then one cannot be held responsible for not having complied with it. So just exactly what is "adultery?"

In Judeo-Greco-Roman times, as in our own, adultery was narrowly defined for some and broadly defined for others. In the Jewish *Mishnah*, adultery was defined in such a way that only women could commit adultery. Men could say that women had somehow seduced them by the clothes they wore or their demeanor and that they could not have helped themselves. Recall that when they brought to Jesus the woman caught in the very act of adultery that no man was presented with her.[51] The Law permitted them to stone her [but not him?]. Had Jesus complied with their rendition of the Law, He would have had to authorize them in their desire to stone her. But can one comply with an unjust Law and retain one's justness? Under the influence of the rabbis, the law held women responsible and left men off the hook. This was certainly not the intent of the Mosaic Law, for both the man and the woman came under the jurisdiction of the Law.[52]

Under Jewish Law, as expressed in the *Mishnah*, divorce had undergone a deviant evolution. Moses seems to have authorized divorce in certain cases. Rabbis Shammai and Hillel differed on the meaning of Moses's sanctioning divorce, one more liberal than the other. As is usually the case—the more liberal the interpretation, the more permissive the policy. Men seized on the opportunity to change their women by adopting the interpretation of the Law that allowed divorce whenever the husband found *any fault* with his wife. In short, as a result of the liberal interpretation of a man's right to divorce his wife, women were victimized. When faced with the prospect of taking a younger, more attractive, and more fecund wife, it becomes easier to discover something offensive in the old one.

Whereas men had a permissive right of divorce, women under Jewish Law had virtually no right of divorce. There were only three conditions under which women *could compel* their husbands to give them a divorce. The conditions were if he was employed as: 1) a copper smelter, 2) a leather

---

51 John 8:1 ff

52 Leviticus 18

tanner, or 3) a dung collector. Two things become immediately evident. First, the phrasing of the law left the power in the hands of the husband. If a man was employed in one of these occupations, *the woman could not divorce him*, but she could *compel him to divorce her.* Second, these divorces have nothing to do with moral treatment. Apparently, having to be intimate with such a man could become too gross for anyone to tolerate, and the Law left a way for the woman to escape this intolerable circumstance.

A close examination of Jesus's words reveals Jesus's value system. First, Jesus is no advocate of the total animality doctrine. He presupposes that each person has the capacity to override any appetite and so has the moral responsibility to do so. Lust is not just an appetite that drives behavior. There is an intervening will whose activity either permits the appetite to proceed unabated or restricts it. Lust is the problem. Without lust, there can be no adultery. Without adultery, there can be no divorce. Nor can there be the sexual victimization of women. In the original language, "looking" is in present tense.[53] That means that the "looking" is ongoing. The verb is also masculine, indicating that the one who is continually looking has a masculine antecedent. A lusting person is one who cannot look at another without assessing that person as a potential sex partner. Once someone "qualifies" as sexually desirable, then the lust-er devises a strategy for consummating the lust. If it becomes physically impossible to complete the lust, the desire to complete it remains. The lust may have to refocus on some other more vulnerable target.

This is what Jesus means by *porneia*, "except for fornication." Refining the law will not alter the character of a person in the least. More and tighter legislation will not alter a person's character, although it may have some effect on modifying behavior. But as we have already seen, for Jesus merely behaving properly is morally insufficient. When the character of a person contains no lust-trait but contains rather a fidelity trait, no law is needed at all. Transform the character trait of lust into the character trait of being a "one-woman man" or a "one-man woman"—not only will there be no adultery, there can be no adultery. This is why fidelity is assured. The condition necessary for infidelity, namely lust, does not exist. Without lust, there can be no *porneia*. Without *porneia,* there is no adultery and so no need for divorce. The surpassing righteousness consists in acquiring the holiness traits that render Law unnecessary or irrelevant.

Second, the verb "commits adultery" has a masculine subject. Recall

53 Matthew 5:28

that the *Mishnah* defined adultery such that only women could commit it. In fact, the section of the *Mishnah* devoted to these matters is entitled "Adulteresses." So Jesus says in effect, "You men are always committing adultery by using your divorce policy as a cover for your lust. You are making the women adulteresses, to the extent that they are." This allegation would cut across the grain of every Jewish male and certainly across the grain of every Jewish rabbi.

This is a long way away from the character of the two Josephs. First, the Joseph of Genesis[54] resisted the advances of Potiphar's wife with the words, "How can I do this evil against my God?" He fled and she, as a woman scorned, made him pay. But he refused to take sexual advantage of a willing, beautiful, and lustful woman. He refused to demean either the dignity of God, her, her husband, or himself. He accepted the responsibility for the moral goodness of himself and the seducing woman. His character made him incapable of consummating this association. The second Joseph was betrothed to Mary, the mother of Jesus.[55] Given her pregnancy and his not being the father, his was a moral dilemma. Should he divorce her? The assurances of the angel helped him to decide, but the anguish he experienced showed the quality of his love for her as well as the character of his integrity. His character defined the nature of his turmoil. Had he no holiness traits, the decision would have been much easier. How does he balance his love for her and for the holiness his God justifiably expects? This Joseph surely exemplifies what Paul meant when he says that the leadership of the church must consist of "one-woman men."[56] It is a quality of a person's character, not the counting of marriage certificates in various courthouses.

"GOD HATES DIVORCE"

Finally, consider a word about the legalistic debate over divorce. It is easy to try to establish the sanctity of marriage by demanding legalistically,

---

54   Genesis 39:1–19

55   Matthew 1:19–20

56   I Timothy 3:2 One of the qualities that Paul requires in the Church's leadership is that leaders must be μιᾶς γυναικὸς ἄνδρα The NIV translates the phrase as "the husband of one wife." This translation prefers a reading that sends the signal that he may have only one wife as a quantity whereas the phrase "one-woman-man" lends itself to construing the relationship in terms of the quality of his commitment to her.

or behaviorally, that all divorce and remarriage is the moral equivalent of adultery. I'm not at all sure about this logic either morally or biblically. I have always found it interesting that the verse "God hates divorce" is quoted as the proof text for justifying the absolute elimination of divorce from Christianity.[57] The prophets are fond of using marriage, infidelity, and divorce to explain God's problem with moral rebellion of Judah and Israel. In fact, in two places, God divorces Israel for her infidelity.[58] Apparently, God—according to the prophets—feels morally justified (indeed, is morally justified) in divorcing someone who goes "whoring after other gods," the moral equivalent of a slut sleeping around on her husband.[59] In fact, God remarries Israel after she repents, in violation of the Law, for no one who divorces a woman is permitted to remarry her.[60] What are we to make of these biblical facts?

Divorcing someone for other than moral reasons is to treat that someone as dispensable. When my daughters were young, there appeared on our doorstep a quite cute kitten. My wife and I are not pet-oriented, so when our daughters found the kitten, the inevitable occurred. We kept the kitten because the girls thought it was so cute and implored us with promises and tears to keep the kitty. A couple of months later, the kitten had grown up enough to notice that "it" was a "he." The cat began to mark "our" house as "his" territory. The cat was fine as an occupant of our house until his animality crossed our values. We did not want to smell the evidence of his attempt to assert his territorial dominance. Nor did we want to spend money to "fix" him. We found the cat another home. We took him to the "humane" society (an interesting term since the cat is not human at all, but humans are expected to treat animals with a modicum of dignity and respect). Whether the cat was adopted or euthanized, I do not know. But neither have I any moral fault nor feel any moral regret for banishing the cat

---

57   See Malachi 2:16—"I hate divorce," says the Lord God of Israel.

58   See Isaiah 50:1 "This is what the LORD says: "Where is your mother's certificate of divorce with which I sent her away?"and Jeremiah 3:8 "I gave faithless Israel her certificate of divorce and sent her away because of all her adulteries. Yet I saw that her unfaithful sister Judah had no fear; she also went out and committed adultery."

59   See the prophet Hosea in this regard.

60   Deuteronomy 24:3–4 "her first husband, who divorced her, is not allowed to marry her again after she has been defiled. That would be detestable in the eyes of the LORD. Do not bring sin upon the land the LORD your God is giving you as an inheritance."

from our home. If, however, I went through the same process of thinking and action-taking with my wife, or she with me, it would be morally outrageous. To discard a human being as cavalierly as one would a cat is demeaning to that human being.

Yet in Jesus's time, this is exactly the power the Law gave to men. Women were the kittens become cats. Jesus summarily condemns both the legalization and practice of cavalier divorce—divorce for the purpose merely of meeting "my needs." People are not animals. Divorce is reserved solely for the dissolution of a marriage *on moral grounds*. And yet, the higher moral order is to grant mercy, grace, and forgiveness when the offending partner repents. This is the lesson of the prophet Hosea. God uses the marriage of Hosea to Gomer as a parable of the relationship He has with a sinfully rebellious people. Hosea is commanded to take Gomer back from her whoring to illustrate the commitment God has to people He loves. But it cannot be ignored that God is perfectly willing to divorce a whoring people on moral grounds, and He is willing to reestablish the relationship when the whore repents.

Jesus sets a high moral standard for marriage and is intolerant of anyone who for any reason demeans the dignity of anyone. The primary relationship of marriage does not reduce to sexual or any other compatibility. The four fundamental holiness values are first expressed in marriages, and if not there, hardly anywhere. Jesus's disciples were so compelled by the moral high ground of His values that they observed that it would be better for a man not to marry at all.[61] Perhaps marriage should be elevated to this moral high ground and then no Law would be needed.

---

61 Matthew 19:10

CHAPTER 7—Beyond the Conventional Wisdom: Keeping Your Word: Matthew 5:33–37

John F. Kennedy wrote a book, the title of which is *Pragmatics*. The premise of the book is that politics is the art of getting things done. In general, this is merely an extension of a uniquely American philosophy, i.e., pragmatism. You will no doubt recognize the names of John Dewey and William James in this connection. Charles Sanders Peirce is less well known but perhaps a bit more important. Pragmatism has a theory of truth. Truth is what works. Whatever achieves the desired result is true. Conversely, if something does not succeed, it is not true. By now, you are starting to think that this is akin to the philosophy, "The ends justify the means." You would be right. Lying can be an effective strategy for success, at least in the short run. And as the eminent twentieth-century economist Lord John Maynard Keynes argued, "In the long run, we're all dead." Lord Keynes had no doubt failed to take into consideration the fact that the resurrection of Jesus assures us that there is indeed a very, very long run!

You recall, however, that the surpassing righteousness consists in rejecting the logic of justification. Surpassing righteousness is doing what is right whether the result brings good or ill to us. Truth happens to be important for its own sake. Someone living a life based on fantasy, well intended or not, is destined, not for success, but for failure in the most significant sense. There is a reason that the Old Testament Law had a threefold formula for truthfulness: 1) do not lie, 2) do not deceive, and 3) do not bear false witness.[62]

---

62 Leviticus 19:11–12

THE LOGIC OF LYING

You have probably thought that using falsehoods is a good thing if telling them brings about a good result. We should not, after all, hurt anyone. Therefore, if the truth will hurt someone, then a falsehood is a good thing. This is the conventional wisdom. This is not the only logic of justification for using falsehoods to succeed. My brother-in-law teaches an adult Sunday school class. One morning, he taught on not lying. During the course of the discussion, the point of which was that Christians ought always to be truthful, one man vehemently objected by saying that if he followed this principle in his business, he would be out of business. Here, pragmatism once again rears its omnipresent head. The objective for this businessman was to do business and make a profit. Since his competitors lied to succeed, he is forced to lie to stay in the game.

The forty-second president of the United States used this logic. He was subpoenaed to testify in a sexual harassment case an Arkansas State employee brought against him. The oath required that he swear to "Tell the truth, the whole truth, and nothing but the truth, so help me God." The intent of this oath is to preserve the Rule of Law, and the Rule of Law depends on the foundation of facts. Those who commit perjury are—or at least, ought to be—subject to severe sanction. When every person is required to be fully truthful in a court of law, the results of deliberation have the best chance of achieving justice (the equal protection of *all* citizens under the Law). If, on the other hand, *some* people, usually the wealthy and powerful, may, at their sole discretion, deviate from, withhold, or distort facts in order to achieve some other success, the Rule of Law and so "equal protection under the Law" is seriously compromised.[63]

The forty-second president used the justification logic (as would most in similar circumstances). Examine his arguments.[64] First, he was justified in

---

63 See Ronald Dworkin *Law's Empire* [Cambridge, MA: Belnap Press of Harvard University, 1986], Chapter Five: "Pragmatism and Personification" for a revealing discussion of the logic of legal pragmatism according to which a judge may exercise his/her legal discretion independently of the constitution or statute or legal precedent and decide a case based solely on his/her assessment of what is in the best interest of the community.

64 For an account of President Clinton's grand jury testimony see: Bob Woodward *Shadow: Five Presidents and the Legacy of Watergate* [New York: Simon & Schuster, 1999], Chapter 35, pp. 430–445. In assessing the President's testimony Charles Bakaly,

being "less than forthcoming" in his testimony because the questions were personally embarrassing. He did not, he said, want to subject his family to public humiliation for his actions. Second, he could not be held responsible for the inability of the plaintiff's attorneys to ask precise enough questions to *force* him to be any clearer than he was. Third, the charges were politically motivated, and so he was forced to frustrate his political opposition. Lying or, as he would say, "not cooperating" in his political demise, was justified. By being completely truthful, he would have compromised his political position. That would have compromised his ability to carry out his agenda for "the good of the American people." The end (retaining political power to advance a political agenda) justifies the means; lying under oath (i.e., perjury) can be pragmatically justified. Finally, he argued that "the American people" in their wisdom did not regard these turpitudes to be sufficiently grievous to overturn an election. In other words, if many or even most people think that someone's lying is justified, that affirms that the lying is indeed pragmatically justified. If holding someone accountable for lying under oath threatens to upset the economy, then it is pragmatically better to let the lie go. If a lie threatens a Constitutional crisis, then swearing to a lie is pragmatically justified. The Senate's voting contrary to the evidence of perjury is pragmatically justified, as well.

During this time, a coworker and I often discussed these matters. She argued each of these points as vociferously as the president had through his lawyers. It was quite frustrating to me because none of these justifications was logically or morally defensible. In one final attempt to break through her logic of justification, I asked whether she thought that had she filed a sexual harassment charge against me, I would be justified in deviating from, withholding, or distorting the facts that were material to her case. Would I be justified in deviating from, withholding, or distorting the facts because my family would be embarrassed? Would I be justified in deviating from, withholding, or distorting the facts because most of the people in the office thought my job performance was too important to jeopardize my employment? Would I be justified in deviating from, withholding, or distorting the facts because she and her friends are merely after me politically? Would she argue each of these points if her daughter were

---

an attorney in Kenneth Starr's Office of Independent Counsel and who had observed the proceeding from the grand jury room, wondered, according to Woodward, "if Clinton were not the perfect liar." *Shadows*, pg. 443

subjected to sexual harassment? Even with these questions on the table, she would assert that "it was different." Apparently, the only reason that "it was different" consisted in that whereas common citizens could not be permitted to avoid testifying truthfully, the president can, presumably due to his privileged status. For this woman, the notion of the Rule of Law was dead. To see if I was right about this, I asked her whether she thought that it was important to have a society based on the Rule of Law. Her response was, "Everybody breaks the law, anyway." At this point, I decided that spending further time and energy trying to be an advocate for what was true, right, and good would be "casting pearls before swine and giving holy things to dogs." We never again broached this subject. God will, however, take it up at some future time.

HWJA—"HOW WOULD JESUS ARGUE?"

This logic is so firmly embedded into the culture and psyche of our world that Jesus's values seem so very unrealistic. Whenever I introduce these matters in my classes, whether in the prison system or in the church, the responses are the same. "If I follow the prescription Jesus sets up, I will become harmed in some way because it only works when *everyone* adheres to the principle. And since *everyone* does not, Jesus is being impractical." Notice the pragmatic logic. A policy is wrong because it fails to produce some intended result. So any policy that achieves some intended result is justified. Lying is both necessary and beneficial whenever it produces desired results, when it is successful. So one hears, "Nobody actually does things this way, nor should they be expected to." It is as if people say, "Chuck, you're right about the moral high ground, but that isn't the world we live in." My response is that "is-ness" does not replace the "ought-ness." It is a sign of the times when felony convicts and churchgoing Christians are skilled at arguing the same logic of justification. A little reflection reveals why it cannot. *If most people sin, sin does not thereby become the moral standard, does it?* The purpose of holiness in practice is to move "what is" so that the "what is" becomes "what ought to be." But surely no one would argue for very long that whatever moral values exist represents what moral values ought to exist.

Swearing an oath to affirm the truth of something is morally removed from the person who forms his/her character so that she/he cannot lie. Swearing an oath is designed to assure that one's testimony is true. Swearing places someone under the threat of some sanction when it is discovered that the testimony was intentionally or maliciously false. Some people need the threat of some sanction in order to provide the extra motivation to be truthful. For such people, and there seem to be many of them, their truthful testimony must be coerced. This is most certainly not a very high standard of holiness. So Jesus argues that those who would be a part of God's Kingdom must be those whose righteousness surpasses the righteousness of those who will tell the truth only under the coercive threat of some sanction.

It really is quite blasphemous for someone to swear in God's name that his/her testimony is true and then give false testimony. If God exists and is just and holy, He is not likely to be impressed by someone who swears by His name to be truthful and then lies in his/her testimony. In fact, if He is just and holy, He will likely be wroth. Consider Jesus's summary condemnation of the morally absurd oath-taking practices among the rabbis of the time.[65] As blasphemous as it is to use God's name to certify one's false testimony (a practice that may even be a blasphemy of the Holy Spirit), it is foolhardy to swear to the truth of one's testimony by appealing to some inanimate artifact, like the Temple or the Temple Altar. The artifact takes on special significance because it has been sanctified. One does not appeal to anything unsanctified to certify that his/her testimony is true. One does not swear by dirt or sludge. One certifies to the truth of one's testimony by appealing to something that stands for or is dedicated to holiness. Something dedicated to the glory of God, sanctified to honor His holiness, is cheapened by swearing to the truth of some falsehood, all of the gold and gifts notwithstanding. This too is blasphemy. But it was common for the rabbis to say that no one was legally compelled to be truthful by swearing by the Temple or the Altar. But one is legally bound by one's oath when swearing by the gold on the Temple or the gift on the Altar. Now, I'm not very bright, but if I wanted to play fast and loose with the truth, I would pay special attention to these legal scholars. Deception will always be worth the risk in swearing to the truth of something by the Temple or the Altar in the off-chance that the one whom I needed to deceive is naïve enough to believe that the Temple or Altar in honor of God binds me to the truth, when *the law* binds me to the truth only by swearing by the gold or the gift. Of course, if I am discovered, I can always say, "Excuse me, I mean 'I swear by the gold on the Temple or the gift on the Altar.'" In other words, I will first

---

65 Matthew 23:16–22

try to deceive without lying, and then only when that deception fails will I resort to what Josiah Royce calls "Intentionally misapplying an ontological predicate" (i.e., lie). The Law establishes a lower standard of truth. I doubt that God will be as easily deceived by legalistic semantic games as my naïve partner may be, the forty-second president notwithstanding.

Jesus argues quite persuasively that I cannot call to certify my deception anyone whose values my deception violates. What level of self-deception is needed for anyone to believe that God is bound by what I promise or that He will certify to my false testimony? My parents assured me that they would never lie for me. They were never bound by my promises. Rather, I was the one who is bound by my own promises. If I promised something to a friend and certified that I would keep that promise based on what my parents would do, I do not thereby bind my parents. It is a good thing I believed that, because it helped me to become as truthful as I am. But inasmuch as I was sure of my parents' assurances that they would not certify my lies, I am even more certain that God is infinitely less likely to do so. Neither God's name nor Heaven, the home of His throne; nor Earth, His footstool, can alter God's inherent justness, truthfulness, or righteousness, our oaths notwithstanding. God is bound by nothing to which I swear. He is bound only by His holiness. I am sure that God will certify and attest to my integrity and truthfulness when it violates nothing of His holiness. Others may be duped by my oaths using these sanctified things to certify them, but God is not. It is an insult to His character and intelligence to think for a nanosecond that He could be. I have never thought it a very good practice to try to deceive someone smarter than I am, just as it is not a very good practice to try to deceive someone about whom God cares very much.

WWJD—WHAT WOULD JESUS DO?

When there is an increase in laws, there has been an increase in immorality. This is true because the righteous man needs no law. The disciple of God's Kingdom surpasses the Law. For the person of holy character, no laws are necessary. The law merely becomes what Paul calls a "tutor" in schooling people in distinguishing the right from the wrong when their maturity is not yet adequate to distinguish good from evil. Law has value, but its value is secondary to the standard of holiness that forms the foundation of the law. So the more holy people become, the more irrelevant the law becomes.

Jesus argues that those people who will populate the Kingdom of Heaven are those whose character surpasses the need for Law.

Jesus sets the standard by saying that the Kingdom disciple's word is transparent. There is always and only a clear connection between the disciple's intentions and actions. "Let your 'yes' be 'yes' and your 'no' be 'no'." There was a time when people jealously guarded their personal integrity. It was important for them to be known as someone whose word was good. People would take a loss in business rather than break their word. There was a need for neither a contract nor a battery of lawyers to intimidate and coerce people into abiding by their word. It was, in fact, an insult to even suggest that a written contract was even an option. *Jesus expects a return to such a standard.*

For anyone who would be a disciple of the Kingdom of Heaven, there is no need to call on holy things to certify one's truthfulness. It matters not whether the laws of perjury apply. Telling the truth or, more precisely, being truthful (I hope that by now you comprehend the difference) occurs independently of the coercive sanctions of the law. No Kingdom disciple will tell the truth in a court of law or on the street because of the threat of perjury. No Kingdom disciple will play fast and loose with the truth when the law is not likely to get involved. The "yes" is always yes, and the "no" is always no. An answer or a testimony will be whatever it is no matter the time or the place or in the presence of whomever. It is inconceivable for anyone to believe that Jesus would stoop to the pragmatic justification of lying in order to establish the truth of something. Jesus would always speak the truth because He is truthful. As John records Jesus saying, "I am the Way, the Truth, and the Life; no one comes to the Father except through Me."[66] He expects His disciples to be truthful. As He is, so I am expected to be.

---

66 John 14:6

CHAPTER 8—Beyond the Conventional Wisdom: The Second Mile: Matthew 5:38–48

When Muslims and Hindus rioted after India's quest for independence was won, the justification was that "it's just an eye for an eye." They are, after all, just getting even. "An eye for an eye makes the whole world blind!" was Mahatma Gandhi's tersely profound commentary on the logic of retaliation. Gandhi was a student of the *Sermon*.

Eschewing retaliation is perhaps the most difficult lesson for a disciple of the Kingdom to learn. Retaliation and revenge perpetuates and accelerates the cycle of violence. The logic of retaliation argues that once some injustice or malice demeans the dignity of me or mine, I am justified in exacting some form of retribution. This is the moral principle of the conventional wisdom. It is even popular to say, "I don't get mad, I get even." As this trips off the tongue, everyone can hear the underlying threat—not of what the words say, but of what the intent is. "You will pay dearly because I am going to be coolly deliberate in devising a way to make your malice toward me or mine very, very costly." There is something more terrifying about someone who acts with cool, calculated malice rather than mere passionate reprisal.

Gandhi learned from Jesus better as a Hindu than we who purport to be His disciples. He transcends Hindu religious teaching and approaches the surpassing righteousness Jesus expects. How can this be? In nearly every discussion I have ever had about Jesus's teaching on this matter of "An eye for an eye," the logic of reprisal battles the logic of surpassing righteousness. Is it morally appropriate to keep back the trump card of revenge just in case we need to play it on the last trick? Is it true that Jesus sets a standard of righteousness that is a wonderful ideal but is essentially impractical? But no impractical ideal is an ideal at all. An ideal must be do-able. Does the fact that most people will refuse to abide by the standard of surpassing righteousness suffice to disqualify the ideal itself? Gandhi did not think so. Can Jesus get only a Hindu sage to agree with Him?

THE LOGIC OF RETALIATION

The Law of Moses established a principle of equity in redressing the effects of malice or negligence. When malice or negligence damages someone, the unreflective reaction is to "make them pay." The Law required that a victim could extract no more from a perpetrator than the damage had caused. This is the intended logic of the "eye for an eye, tooth for tooth." But there is also anger at someone's attempt to damage me or mine even when a malicious attempt fails. The Law of Moses made no provision for either punitive damages or for pain and suffering. The Law required that the one offended or damaged be put back into the condition he was prior to the damaging event, or else to damage the damager no further than the damage he caused.

This principle's sole purpose was to make sure that the cycle of violence could not get started and, if started, could not continue. As a rational principle, it stands very well, yet there is an asymmetry between the exactitude of the Law and the assuagement of an anger or hurt. This is no doubt the reason that punitive damages and awards for pain and suffering crept into the law. Perhaps people thought that an extreme punishment would perform a couple of functions. The law provided for economic and psychic punishment, a monetary cost as well as a cost in shame and embarrassment. First, it would help to manage the wrath of the offended. Second, it would also inflict a punishment sufficient to guarantee that people would take responsibility for the effects of their actions whether intended or unintended. If there were malicious intent, the malice would become very expensive, both economically and psychically. If there were merely negligence, it would provide the incentive to be more reflective. Repayment or restoration serves as the economic cost and sacrificial atonement as the psychic cost: public shame and personal guilt.

But what happens when the person harmed by some wrong is not or cannot be assuaged by the principle of legal equity? The principle of equity in Law is that people should be restored to the previous condition. This is easier said than done. Some things are damaged or destroyed which have more than economic value. How does one restore the loss of a bodily function? What is the restorative remedy when negligence or malice leaves someone paralyzed or without a limb or spouseless or childless? How can irreversibly damaged things or people be replaced? What if someone, through negligence or malice, destroys anything irreplaceable? How does one replace property that has little economic value but significant personal value, such as some memento of a significant event, a gift or photo, or letters and cards? Things that have merely economic value can be replaced by an economic settlement, but it becomes an insult to reduce the value of irreplaceable things by giving such things mere economic value. The presumption that it is possible or equitable to do so creates even more hostility and resentment than the loss itself. It is here more than anywhere else that the cycle of retaliation begins. "If I can make you hurt as badly as your negligence or malice has hurt me, then I will feel better."

DYNAMIC BALANCE

Surely, no one can disagree with the moral principle that those who harm others should not get away with their actions. To allow people to get away with harming others would hasten the disintegration of social cohesion by damming up resentment. This is the reason for the principle of advocacy. Everyone has the moral responsibility for being an advocate for what is true, right, and good, just as everyone has the moral responsibility for moral goodness in him/herself and others. To be an advocate for the true, right, and good requires that people insert themselves into the circumstance in which someone is demeaning someone else. This is not retaliation. It is restraining or diverting and perhaps even accepting the malice of one person against another. But in addition to the third principle, there is the fourth. Without the fourth principle, that everyone has the moral responsibility for being proactive in the reconciliation of everyone to God and to each other, there can be no stopping the cycle of violence and reprisal. This principle prevents advocacy from becoming retaliation. Everyone has the responsibility for being proactive in reconciling people to each other. Preserving, or trying to preserve, the dignity of everyone becomes a balancing act. To allow someone to get away with demeaning another means that two are demeaned—both the perpetrator and the victim. Advocacy tips the balance toward the one who is exploited or demeaned. Reconciliation tips the balance back toward the perpetrator.

Jesus treads on difficult ground here. He presents the logic of surpassing righteousness by saying that anyone who would become a disciple of God's Kingdom must have the character to accept that being wronged, even wronged irreparably, is no justification for perpetuating the logic of reprisal. There is a very good reason for this. The hurts we experience are often qualitatively different than the possible legal remedies. The Law is inherently incapable of remedying psychological hurt or irreparable physical damage, damage to one's reputation and integrity, or damage to those we love and respect. But the answer to the redress of these kinds of damage is not to create some counterbalancing irreparable damage on the principle of "an eye for an eye." Let's say that someone has killed a child by drunk driving. Now the principle of "an eye for an eye" *seems* to permit the killing of the perpetrator's child by running over it with a car. (Of course, we do not go this far, but we would like to find a way to punish this perpetrator with the same pain we experience.) Causing him/her a similar pain is clearly extreme, although in many places in the world, killing women and children is justified on this principle—as in terrorism, for example. I pick this extreme example to illustrate how the logic of retaliation is so flawed. No one with a moment of rational reflection will think that this is in any way equitable, even if the perpetrator experiences the same hurt as she/he caused. Innocent third parties should not have to suffer loss in order to inflict similar suffering on someone else. Besides, the ripple effects of this kind of retaliation damages far more people than the perpetrator. But there are several other reasons for this. She/he may have no children. The drunk may be so insensitive that she/he cares nothing for his/her children, or at least cares for his/her children less than you do. My daughter once had boss whose fifteen-year-old son had the symptoms of Hodgkin's disease. His alcoholic mother would not go to the hospital to be with him on the day a biopsy would be taken because she "had some shopping to do." Such levels of insensitivity are inconceivable to Kingdom disciples. My daughter was angry at this mother's indifference, and she hurt for the father. But even her anger and hurt could not approach the absolute and justifiable anger and inconsolable hurt this father had. There is here an incredible temptation to "make her pay for her indifference." What she is doing is not illegal, but it is a long way from being moral.

If the cycle of retaliation has to stop in examples as extreme as these, it will absolutely have to stop for less extreme, even petty situations. Considered alongside examples of extreme malice, terrorism, or criminal exploitation, many of the indignities we experience are incredibly trivial. Indeed, many churches experience only trivial indignities. Rudeness, insensitive treatment, being politically victimized, or merely being overlooked in some regard is hardly adequate reasons for the levels of retaliation that occur. A teacher does not appeal to us, or a program leaves my child out, or a preacher's sermons are "not meeting my needs" hardly justify trying to get people fired or spreading malicious gossip or striving to create embarrassing dissension and division. Certainly that the building committee chooses a carpet of the wrong color does not warrant the anger and resentment it often does. Anyone who believes that resentment and retaliation over such trivialities is justified is no candidate for the Kingdom of Heaven. Righteousness must be surpassing.

VICTIMS, PERPETRATORS, AND ADVOCATES

At some point, the cycle of retaliation has to stop. As Gandhi so profoundly argued, "An eye for an eye makes the whole world blind." It is said that Gandhi was heavily influenced by the *Sermon*. I am constantly amazed that "the little brown man in a loincloth" seems to comprehend the length, depth, and breadth of Jesus's teaching more than any Christian I have ever talked to about it. How is it that this remarkable Hindu man can comprehend Jesus's *Sermon*, while we Christians continue to hold back the trump card of retaliation to play when everyone else is out of trump?

For Jesus, the surpassing righteousness is expressed in the willingness of God's disciple to experience wrong or harm or exploitation without reprisal. It means going the second mile. There are generally three roles, not just two, in any circumstance of harm or exploitation. In thinking only about the perpetrator and the victim, we leave out of consideration the role of the advocate. This is unfortunate and devastating in the battle of good against evil. Rather than a dyadic model for describing this relationship, we must adopt a triadic model. In this model, there are three distinct elements in a dynamic relationship. First, there is the *Perpetrator*. This is someone or some group whose activities or policies demean the dignity of another person or group. Second, a perpetrator needs a victim. A *Victim* is someone or some group whose dignity is being demeaned by another person or group. The third element—often overlooked, neglected, or ignored—is the advocate. An *Advocate* is anyone who accepts his/her responsibility for coming to the aid or defending the dignity of any person or group who is being demeaned.

Jesus's teaching here is often interpreted in dyadic terms. He seems to address the situation in which there is only a victim and a perpetrator. Taking this dyadic orientation, the teaching requires that the victim does not resist being exploited or oppressed. Because of this dyadic view, many people either say that Jesus could not mean this, or if He does mean it, He expects something unrealistic. Surely, one can never advocate passivity for anyone who is being exploited. Surely one is justified in defending oneself against any demeaning or exploitative activity! In all my years of being a student of the Bible and of Christianity, I could never make sense of this teaching until I understood a scene in the movie *Gandhi*.[67] When Gandhi was accused of advocating "passive resistance," he responded that he had never advocated "passive" anything. Gandhi and an English clergyman are walking down a street in South Africa. As they walk along, it becomes clear that they will have to pass by a group of street thugs. The clergyman begins to turn aside to avoid the inevitable confrontation, a confrontation that is more than likely to produce a beating. Gandhi asks whether Jesus meant what He said about not resisting evil. The clergyman says that he thinks Jesus is "being somewhat metaphorical." Gandhi argues that in being an advocate for what is true, right, and good, one must receive a blow—perhaps many blows—in order to show that you will not be turned aside. Nor will you engage in violence. Gandhi argues that when one takes this stance, the anger and hostility of the perpetrator decreases, and his respect for you increases. The amazing characteristic of Gandhi's argument is that the dignity of both the perpetrator and the victim is recognized, that the reconciliation of the victim and the perpetrator must be achieved if at all possible.

But, even in this case, the advocate is present. The advocate is present in the victim. So whether or not the advocate is present in the person of the third party, she/he is always present in the person of the victim. Gandhi says he is always an advocate of fighting. He just requires that fighting never resort to violence. Violence jeopardizes the ability to achieve reconciliation. Advocacy for the true, right, and good must be dynamically balanced with dignity and respect as well as reconciliation. The three roles must be balanced as a tightrope walker must keep himself in the center of the vertical and horizontal and lateral forces that threaten to plunge him in a crushing plummet to the ground. To illustrate, consider a hostage situation.

---

67   Briley, *Gandhi* pg. 22-23

Someone threatens to harm another and you, as a third party, have to balance these four values between these three roles. In order to achieve a just resolution of this situation, do the hostage and the perpetrator deserve equal dignity treatment? Decidedly not, for in taking these actions, the perpetrator has dealt away some of his/her dignity in taking and holding the victim hostage. If the perpetrator is at all worth being reconciled, she/he must be prevented from doing harm or from being harmed by the exercise of "undue force." But to create a situation that achieves that objective requires that the preservation of the victim's dignity take a higher priority. So the advocate will have to stop the assault without harming either party if possible, but by harming only the perpetrator if necessary. This principle is at the core of hostage negotiation. To resolve the conflict nonviolently is the highest good.

Consider what the hostage negotiator will sometimes do. She/he will attempt to exchange him/herself for the hostage, subjecting him/herself to harm in order to remove the victim from harm's way. The role of an advocate now has changed the dynamics of the situation by forcing the perpetrator to now harm someone who is no longer an involuntary victim but a voluntary one. The dynamics have changed. It becomes much more difficult for someone to engage in evil the more innocent the victim is.

Gandhi comprehended this insight from Jesus. Jesus's crucifixion is the acme of this principle. Only those who are incredibly evil will murder an innocent man whose only crime is that He went around doing good, advocating goodness, and being good. Paul takes up the same principle by saying, "If your enemy hungers, give him something to eat. If he is thirsty, give him something to drink, for in so doing, you heap coals of fire on his head."[68] Peter expresses the principle by saying in his first epistle that no Christian should suffer from doing anything morally wrong.[69] If we are to suffer, let it be because we are righteous, not because we are lawless. Early Christians were persecuted terribly, but were always willing to expose brutality by experiencing exploitation publicly. Let no one perpetrate evil in secret. Let all men see it publicly in the full light of the street. Martin Luther King's efforts were the more powerful because the television cameras showed a passive and apathetic world the brutality of a racism that would use fire hoses and attack dogs on unarmed nonviolent protestors. "Let your

68 Romans 12:20

69 I Peter 2:11–12

light so shine before men that they may see your good works and glorify your Father who is in Heaven."[70] Being innocently demeaned and abused carries its own moral persuasion. At the foot of the cross, the anonymous Roman soldier gazed on the crucified Jesus and could only deduce, "Truly, this man was the Son of God."[71]

---

70   Matthew 5:16

71   Matthew 27:54

CHAPTER 9—"Be Ye Perfect . . ."— Coming Full Circle: Matthew 5:43–48

Nothing is as pernicious as the popular contemporary view that man is incapable of moral perfection. One of the first classes I ever took in Bible College was a required course in the Gospels. When the time came for us to consider the *Sermon*, I was amazed (and am still amazed) that we would spend time considering whether Jesus meant what He plainly said. "Be ye therefore perfect as your Father in heaven is perfect."[72] I apparently persist in making the mistake of believing what my home church had taught me. I believed that the Bible was inspired and, therefore, was literally true. Jesus must have meant what He said, since what He said was included in the Bible. Imagine my consternation and confusion when this professor of Bible, as I now realize was playing the Devil's Advocate, began telling me that no man could comply with this apparent directive, since man is a sinner and can only be "declared righteous" in virtue of Christ's death on the cross. I could never make the leap from this moral expectation of perfection to imputed righteousness. How could an actual sinner become imputedly righteous?

I could not then see, nor can I see now, how a moral imperative could be satisfied by anyone other than by an individual person. The moral purity of one person is not something that can be imputed to another. The prophet Ezekiel effectively addresses the danger of this kind of reasoning.[73] Each person is either righteous or not based what she/he has become and what

---

72 Matthew 5:48 recalling Leviticus 19:2

73 Ezekiel 18:4, 20 "The soul that sins is the one that will die."

she/he has done alone. One can neither defend himself against being held morally responsible nor be morally praised by appealing to the actions of his father or his son. It is like reasoning that since my father was a good man, he may impute to me his goodness, a goodness that I do not have on my own. Many kids think this way. They end up becoming amoral brats. It is much easier to say that you must regard me as good because my father is good than it is for me to accept responsibility for being good myself.

Jesus does *not* say in Matthew 5:48, "Because your Father in Heaven is perfect, or because His Son is, you can be *regarded* as perfect." Nor does He say that you can be *regarded* as perfect in virtue of His loving you, as the death of His Son on the cross putatively declares. Does not anyone think, as I do, that there is something peculiar about God's saying, if He does, that since His Son is morally perfect, and you and I are not, that He is going to *regard* you or me as perfect in virtue of His Son's perfection in spite of the fact that we are sinners? If this was true, it is difficult to see how anyone could avoid becoming a universalist, i.e., believing that God saves everyone He loves independently of his or her sin. Jesus's statement is in the form of a holiness imperative. He says, quite plainly, "Be ye therefore perfect, as your Father in heaven is perfect."

Is Man Morally Impotent?

The clear implication of the popular theology is that man is morally impotent. But why should we suppose that he is? By morally impotent, I mean what Augustine said in this regard. Augustine said that man is "not able not to sin" [*non posse non peccare*] merely by virtue of being human. If someone is morally impotent, it means that if someone is a human being then, as a human being, it is not possible for such a one to go through life, no matter how long or short it may be, without committing at least one sin. The reason Augustine and the Reformers believed that this is true is that they believed that human beings carry an *inherited* trait due to the fall of Adam. All Catholics and many others call this "original sin."[74] Reformers call this attribute "total depravity." It all comes to the same thing logically.

---

74 Thomas Aquinas believed this so thoroughly that it presented a problem for him in accounting for the sinlessness of Jesus. He finally explained the moral purity of Christ by arguing that the original sin trait came from the male and since Jesus had no human father, He escaped inheriting original sin. "Original sin is transmitted to the children not by the mother, but by the father." *Summa Theologica* [Part I of Second Part Q. 81 Article 5]

If one sins because of some *inherited* trait, then one cannot be held morally responsible for the actions that occur in virtue of that trait. It is like holding people as morally deficient because they are of a certain race (something Christians have unfortunately argued in the past).

The Reformers, following Augustine's lead, argued on three grounds that man could have no free will without demeaning the dignity of God and the value of His *grace*. The following represents the character of their reasoning.

1. *The Power Argument.* If there is such a thing as free will among men, then there is a power in man such that it is sufficient to conquer sin. But the only power sufficient to conquer sin is the power of God's grace. Therefore, there is no free will, and for anyone to claim that there is nullifies the grace of God, for then there would be two powers in virtue of which man could conquer his sin—man's free will, on the one hand, and God's grace on the other. This, Martin Luther says, violates the clear teaching of Scripture.

2. *The Impotence Argument.* The more decadent man is, the greater God is. If there were such a thing as free will in man, then man would not be as decadent or impotent as if there were no free will, and so God's glory would be lessened as well as the power of His grace.

3. *The Merit Argument.* If anyone is to be saved, then it can only be due either to man's doing something to merit this salvation, putting God under obligation, or else he does not, or as Luther says, cannot do anything to merit it. If man cannot merit salvation, then it is God's grace alone that is the means of his salvation.

But "Ought" implies "Can"!

There are significant problems with each of these arguments. I will avoid the temptation to delve into those problems. I will say, though, that I am always quite astounded that most people, nearly universally so, fail to consider the logical connection between "free will" and "moral responsibility." There can be no moral responsibility for any action over which one has no volitional control. Consider that someone ties me up, wires my hand up to the trigger of a shotgun, attaches electrodes to my arm, and then ties you up in a chair in front of the gun. Now I am told, "Do not pull the trigger, or we will hold you responsible for killing this person." Now, the wires to my arm are touched to a battery, my finger muscles contract around the trigger, the gun discharges, and you are killed. The question is not "Are you killed?" but "Are you murdered?" The former condition is involuntary and is, therefore, not a moral matter. Murder is entirely voluntary if I am to be held morally, and legally, responsible for your death. Remove the notion of free will, and the notion of moral responsibility vanishes. If there is no action in virtue of a free will, then there is no action for which I can be held morally responsible; so there is no action for which I may be justly condemned. I cannot be morally condemned for killing the person in front of the shotgun simply because I had no volitional control over the actions of my body. They were sufficiently controlled by factors over which I had no control whatsoever. As unfortunate as your death is, I am not morally responsible.

Sin vanishes with the banishment of free will. Sin is a moral notion. "To sin" has to mean that someone "voluntarily chooses to violate some principle of moral obligation." If it does not mean this, then "sin" is merely a term that describes certain kinds of involuntary actions, since all actions are *ipso facto* involuntary. There is another consequence of this belief. When sin vanishes with the banishment of free will, then so too do the notions of "perfection" and "holiness." In fact, if God should hold me, or anyone else for that matter, morally responsible for "involuntary" sins (if there can be such a thing), then God becomes unjust and, therefore, loses His claim to be holy, i.e., morally perfect. He becomes no longer worthy of worship, except to do so as a means of pandering to His power (and even this cannot be an act of free will, creating a monumental cognitive inconsistency). Of course, another consequence is that any act of worship cannot be free since no acts are free; all actions are sufficiently conditioned by the will of God.

But Jesus has said, "Be ye therefore perfect as your Father in heaven is perfect." Such a statement of moral imperative can mean only that God is morally perfect and that any Kingdom disciple must become so as well. To say that someone "ought" to do something requires that that someone "can" do the thing she/he "ought to" do. *"Ought" implies "can."* To require an "ought" in the absence of a "can" is unjust. Jesus's comment recalls the commandment God gives in Leviticus 19:2, also quoted by Peter,[75] "You shall be holy, because the Lord your God is holy." Try as we might to avoid being held morally responsible for both moral perfection and for sin, we

---

75 I Peter 1:16

can only do so by sacrificing the holiness of God on the altar of moral impotency. As for me, this consequence comes a bit too close to blasphemy for me to be at all comfortable with it.

LOVE AND FREE WILL

These same people who argue according to Luther's reasoning fail to consider another consequence of this pernicious doctrine. If there is no free will, what can love [ἀγάπη] mean? Is love volitional? Is love a choice, a decision upon which we may act, upon which we are morally obligated to act? Either the answer is "yes" or it is "no." If the answer is "no," then love loses its essential quality. It becomes merely a byproduct of certain blood or brain chemistry or of one's environment. It is merely an appetite. But this is contrary to Jesus's plain teaching in the *Sermon*. Jesus says that it is a decision one is morally obligated to make. Recall that *"ought" implies "can."* If one *ought* to love one's enemies as well as one's friends, then one *can* love one's enemies as well as one's friends. Whether this act of volition occurs or not is a function not of one's appetites or biology or environment, but of one's will.

Jesus points out that the dominant moral value of His environment is that one ought to love one's neighbor but that one is not morally obligated to love an enemy. In fact, this seems an entirely plausible doctrine. It is so plausible a doctrine that few will even consider the surpassing righteousness position, i.e., loving one's enemies. Jesus comments further that it is easy to love those who love you—even pagans can do that. The love of which He speaks is the love that volitionally undertakes actions that are in the beneficial interests of one's neighbor, even should that neighbor be someone who persecutes, reviles, and despises you.

We need to do bit of work unpacking the notion of love, i.e., *agape*. For this, we have to return to the time when the Jewish people decided to translate the Old Testament from Hebrew into Greek. There was a considerable amount of space devoted to disclosing the love of God in the Old Testament.[76] The prevailing Hebrew terms are *ahab* and *chesed*. The predominant Greek term for love in Greek society was *eros*. *Eros* meant "to satisfy one's own needs or desires first." It was then, as it is now, associated

---

76 See: Ethelbert Stauffer ἀγαπάω *Theological Dictionary of the New Testament* Translated & Edited by Geoffrey Bromily [Grand Rapids, MI: Wm B. Eerdman's Pubishing Co, 1964], Vol I, pg. 35 ff.

with sexual activity. What is important for this idea of love is that one experience ecstasy, happiness, pleasure (orgasm, if you will).

The problem that presented itself for the Septuagint translators was that if they chose to use *"eros"* for *"ahab"* or *"chesed,"* they would be creating the impression that God's love is erotic, i.e., that it only seeks its own gratification. This is, of course, completely unacceptable. What was to be done? The solution presented itself when they decided to choose to use an obscure Greek term, *agape*. "Agape" comes to mean "doing what produces holiness in oneself and in others." So, rather than a notion of love that focuses on the self and the aggrandizement of its appetites, *agape* focuses on the moral well-being of the self and others.

In general, the notion of *eros* is "you exist for me." A little reflection reveals that consistently applying *eros* as a philosophy of life can only create dysfunction, exploitation, and results in alienation. In order to have a "you exist for me" relationship, one must be in a relationship. But the essence of such a relationship is that "as soon as you stop meeting my needs, you're history; our relationship is over." When the essence of the relationship is that one's own appetitive needs are primary, and the appetitive needs of all others are secondary, one or the other of the people in the relationship will be jettisoned while the other initiates another "you exist to meet my needs" relationship. This new relationship partner *will be used* until she/he no longer "meets my needs." That relationship will be terminated, and on the cycle endlessly goes. The misguided attempt to love in order to be loved—unintentionally, perhaps—makes enemies and resentment increase geometrically. In the end, there can only be islands of alienated people, each of whom are enemies of all the others. People who are committed to never being used again populate each island. Yet they sally forth to other islands to engage in shallow self-deception and the deception of the other, only to discover again after some period of time that "my needs are not being met." So we again retreat to our island for a while and then sally forth to another one to repeat the process all over again.

When this is everyone else's life philosophy, must we play the same game? Must we trade *agape* for some modicum of short-term *eros*? Must it be that all one can expect from life is a life of lurching from one abusive relationship to another? Jesus says not, but He argues in a very surprising way. *He requires that we agape those people who eros us.* In order to bring *agape* into a world of *eros*, someone must accept the risk of abuse, exploitation, and alienation in order to express *agape*. *Agape* is "love that strives for the holiness of the other." "Love your neighbor as yourself"[77] means the same thing as our second value, "every person is responsible for holiness in oneself and in others." It says that, as a philosophy of life, "I exist to become holy and to bring you to holiness." *Agape* is the willingness to be used in order to become an influence for the moral goodness of others.

This is a remarkably high standard of righteousness. It is not cynical. It does not concede that *eros* is all I can expect, so I must be better at disguising my erotic values in order to get my needs met. It concedes that most people are selfishly looking for relationships that "meet my needs." But it enters into these relationships as a strategy for revealing a more substantial and higher quality relationship. It is surprising to find people who exist for the moral betterment of another. The quality of such a love is overwhelmingly superior. So, as Jesus says, "Love your enemy." "Pray for your enemy." "Work for the good of your enemy."

There is no moral courage in loving those who love us. This is easy. People can easily stay in relationships in which their needs are met. It is easy to return love to people who love you. In dysfunctional relationships, this is called codependency. It is not a good thing, even though one may be comfortable with the arrangement. The basis of all such relationships is an exchange relationship. We agree to reciprocate. "I will enable your irresponsibility if you will enable mine."

The real moral courage consists in what some have called "tough love." If we permit some loved one to persist in irresponsibility, moral or otherwise, we cannot *agape* him/her. When we permit another to persist in irresponsibility, we demean our own dignity for we collapse in the face of a moral crisis. We rank our own psychological comfort or economic well-being ahead of the moral well-being of another. This is just as morally harmful to an enemy as it is to a family member. Love, *agape*, cannot be like this. To conduct life this way violates every one of the four fundamental values. It violates the dignity of people and shows them no respect, for we tolerate their being less than what they are capable of being. It certainly does not promote moral goodness in either oneself or others, for it turns a blind eye to moral turpitude. It is by no means an advocacy for what is true, right, and good, for it does not want to risk a loss to gain goodness. It is hardly proactive in the reconciliation of every person to God and to others,

---

77 Leviticus 19:18. Jesus calls this the second great command in the Law. Paul calls it the fulfillment of the law of Christ.

for it stands for nothing but the satisfaction of the self and its perceived needs. *Eros* only cares about "getting one's own needs met." *Eros* is, in short, demeaning to both oneself and to others. God cannot permit it and also, as John says, "Be love."[78]

When Jesus speaks of loving one's neighbors, even one's enemies—the paradigm changes. One must act in the holiness well-being of everyone. This is *agape*. This is the nature of God's love, and so it becomes the moral standard for the love of *surpassing* righteousness. It is clearly a *surpassing* righteousness. And one more remarkable transformation has occurred. The last of these illustrations of *surpassing* righteousness exactly reverses the first legal compliance. Whereas Jesus begins by saying that one is legally obligated not to murder anyone, He ends by requiring that the *surpassing* righteousness consists in loving one's enemies. A complete transformation has occurred. Only those who satisfy the moral conditions of a *surpassing* righteousness can enter God's Kingdom. Love is an act of the will, not the effusion of the emotions. "Verily, verily I say to you, love your enemies and pray for those who persecute you; thus you will become the sons of your Father who is in heaven."[79]

---

78 I John 4:8, 16

79 Matthew 5:44

CHAPTER 10—Beyond Doing the Right Things: Matthew 6:1–18

"Toot your own horn, or your horn will go untooted!"

I write a very bad résumé. It is not that there is little to put in it. It is just that I find no good reason to sprinkle inappropriate superlatives into it. I am not, after all, omnicompetent. It seems inappropriate to use superlatives at all. If everyone who writes a résumé implies she/he is omnicompetent, there is little to distinguish the hyperbolic prevarication from the real "omnicompetent." Such résumés become effectively useless. Joe Friday's advice is "Just the facts, Ma'am." I guess I think that whatever praise may be due to me or my work should come from some source other than me. A friend of mine says that this is the reason I do not get interviews. He then quotes the heading of this section to me.

But we shall return to the point at hand. It would be rather easy to conclude that since character is the basis of action that one should only take action when one's character and motivations are moral or holy. *Doing* what is right has a certain level of moral value. Indeed, *doing* what is morally right is *necessary* for *being* a holy person. But *doing* what is morally right is not for that reason *sufficient* for *being* a holy person. No one is justified in waiting around for morality in character to strike out of the blue before she/he acts morally. Surpassing righteousness consists in being holy in character as well as behavior. In fact, Jesus understands that when one is holy in character, one's behavior will be righteous. The converse is not true. As the disciple grows from moral infancy to moral maturity,[80] his/her behavior is reinforced by the discipline to do what is not yet natural. Discipline is doing what is right even though it is inconsistent with our level of comfort or willingness. Discipline places the *mind* in a position to dictate an action that is not yet in character. Early in the maturation process, this discipline is external. It exists outside the person, but it becomes morally worthwhile only when it becomes internalized. When this happens, one reaches what Soren Kierkegaard calls "the Knight of Faith."

Consider three types of people who *do* what is right. Assess the moral ranking for each type. First, consider the person who *does* what is right because she/he is afraid of being punished for not *doing* it. Next, consider the person who *does* what is right because she/he wants to receive some blessing or reward. Finally, consider the person who *does* what is right for its own sake, independently of any consideration of rewards or punishments. I use this exercise in my prison classes. The logic of morality is so compelling that they successfully rank them. The morally superior person does what is right independently of rewards or punishments; she/he *does* so for the sake of the good itself. In fact, a person who does what is right even when there is the prospect of experiencing pain or harm ranks even higher. The person who *does* what is right when tempted by some pleasure to do something wrong also expresses the surpassing righteousness. In short, ranking of these types of people requires that character and motivations take a primary role. For people who consider morality or holiness to be merely right actions must argue that all of these moral circumstances have the same moral standing. This is just counterintuitive.

THREE ILLUSTRATIONS

In this next section of the *Sermon,* Jesus provides us with three illustrations of the principle that the disciple's righteousness is a surpassing righteousness when the motivations of right behavior are untainted. The three illustrations cover 1) giving of alms, 2) praying, and 3) fasting. In each case, Jesus expects disciples to engage in the practice but with the understanding that doing

---

80 Consider Hebrews 5:11–14, especially 14, "who by constant use have trained themselves to distinguish between good and evil." The reflexive voice here is telling. It is not passive voice which would mean that someone else trained them to distinguish good from evil. The reflexive reveals the role of initiative in accepting the responsibility for becoming as holy as God justifiably expects.

right things has spiritual (i.e., moral) value only when doing them occurs independently of receiving some praise or reward. Holiness means doing what is right even should there be no prospect of a reward or when doing so may produce pain, punishment, or sanction. *Faith becomes doing what is true, right, and good whether one's life goes well or ill.* Faith is about moral character more than it is about what or how one knows about spiritual things.

I have ministered in a few churches and worked in other capacities in other churches. I have discovered that the easiest way to get chewed out is to omit acknowledging some person for his/her work or contribution to the church. For some people, contributing to the church program or church budget is a trump card to be used in getting one's way in church politics. For such people, there is always a veiled (and sometimes not-so-veiled) threat that if things do not go the way they want them to go, these contributions will dry up.

One church receives memorial gifts from people when a church member dies. The gifts are generally quite modest, usually around $25. But if, for some reason, the gift is misapplied or an acknowledgement is a bit less than timely or not quite public enough, there will be expressions of displeasure ranging from a phone call asking questions to tirades about ingratitude. I frankly fail to understand this self-serving superficiality. The last time I checked this passage, God who sees what is done in secret rewards people openly. But for those who seek effusive public praise for their gifts—that praise is all that they can expect.

People often give to charities including the church (perhaps, especially the church) for all kinds of nonaltruistic reasons. The larger the "gift," the greater is the expected fanfare. Charitable giving, like political giving, is less about promoting ideals and being benevolent than about buying influence or basking in accolades. The less the fanfare, the more is the petulance. What does someone really purchase with the "gift?" The gift implores another to toot an untooted horn.

Jesus exposes this in goring the pharisaical sacred cows. The Pharisees designed their "acts of altruism" for maximum public effect. Their gifts were announced with trumpet fanfare, their prayers waxed eloquent, and their fasting required makeup and acting lessons. Jesus had no doubt frequently seen these three egregious and garish practices. They no doubt really angered Him whenever He saw them. It was surely a source of ridicule by the masses it was designed to impress. People can usually see through such self-aggrandizing practices. So not only do they fail to impress God, they are generally a source of derision displayed behind givers' backs.

Almsgiving—Benevolence with an Altruistic Purpose

The Law had always made provision for taking care of those who were on the economic margins of society, but benevolence never exchanged dignity for financial assistance. It is demeaning for someone to beg for sustenance. The Law provided that those who owned a field could neither go over a field twice, nor could they harvest in the corners of the fields and vineyards. This policy preserved the dignity of the working poor. The surpassing righteousness displays compassion for its own sake. Benevolence strives for the moral goodness of the poor with the understanding that laziness and ingratitude are sins too. Giving alms to the poor is being an advocate for what is true, right, and good. It achieves reconciliation by making sure that just as there is no favoritism for the wealthy, neither is there partiality for the poor. The Law of Moses, as Jesus was always reminding people, required loving one's neighbor as oneself.[81] Love, *agape*, seeks holiness both in self and others. The surpassing righteousness requires that *agape* become more than an externally imposed command. It must become a trait of character.

Prayer—Focusing on God's Will

Think about where and how people learn to pray. If someone is lucky, family prayers will become the model. Generally, the model of family prayer comes from ready-made grace prayers said at meals or bedtime prayers taken from children's books or from books of prayers provided by theologically correct clergy. The other models for saying prayers comes from hearing people pray in public. Most often, such prayers are those we hear in worship services or in study groups. There are two general types of prayers we hear in these environments. First, there is the rote prayer. This is the prayer in which there are *words with little thought*. There are prayers calling on God to do things in generic categories. Prayers like these are prayers of *words without thought*. The words are vain babbling. Second, there is the eloquent prayer. This prayer is replete with "thees" and "thous." They contain flowery eloquence, no doubt the product of much *poetic* planning, but they contain *little thought about holiness*. These prayers are also vain babbling.

We learn what to pray for in similar ways. Before some time devoted to prayer, someone asks for "prayer concerns." Then we make a list of people who are sick or in some personal distress. We then pray for them. We ask God

---

81 Leviticus 19:18 again.

to do something for us, i.e., we ask Him to heal our infirmities or alleviate our distresses. In short, we learn most about intercessory prayer. Intercessory prayer is good, if it meets certain conditions. One must think about what it is appropriate to ask for in an intercessory prayer, or else it too becomes vain babbling. What makes a prayer vain babbling? A prayer is vain babbling when it utters words without thinking about holiness. So then, what *thought* must go into a prayer? Jesus provides the answers in His model prayer.

There are five parts to prayer that babbles not. First, one must think about God's holiness ["Hallowed be Thy name"]. Second, once reminded that God is holy, we commit ourselves to God's will becoming reality ["Thy Kingdom come, Thy will be done on earth as it is in heaven"]. Third, we are permitted to ask for the provisions of the day ["Give us this day our daily bread"]. Fourth, we make a commitment to the reconciliation of others to God. ["Forgive us our debts, as we have also forgiven those who owe us"]. Finally, we pray for God's attendance with us in living out a holy life ["Lead us not into temptation, but deliver us from evil"].

1. God's Holiness—"Our Father Who art in Heaven, hallowed be Thy name"

Since God is holy, it makes no sense to think that He will honor any request that would require Him to act in a way that is inconsistent with that holiness. Every prayer must begin by reminding ourselves of to whom it is we pray. God, who is holy, must be asked only for assistance in taking up holy causes. No one who forgets God's holiness can expect any of his/her prayers to be answered, even if God should choose to hear them. It is good to remember that God has warned repeatedly that people who pray and also act with moral disregard cannot expect to have their prayers even heard.[82] To Jeremiah[83] and to Isaiah[84] God says, "There is no point in this people praying, for I am not listening." No prayer that asks for unholy things will be answered. So think about to whom we pray. If our prayers

---

82 Deuteronomy 29:19

83 Jeremiah 7:16 "So do not pray for this people nor offer any plea or petition for them; do not plead with me, for I will not listen to you." Jeremiah 14:11 "Then the Lord said to me, 'Do not pray for the well-being of this people; though they fast, I will not listen to their cry; though they offer burnt offerings and grain offerings, I will not accept them. Instead I will destroy them with the sword, famine and plague."

84 Isaiah 1:15 "When you spread out your hands in prayer, I will hide my eyes from you; even if you offer many prayers, I will not listen. Your hands are full of blood."

were incompatible with God's holiness, it would be better to not pray at all than to pray blasphemously.

2. God's Will—"Thy Kingdom come, Thy will be done on earth as it is in heaven"

Just as God's Will, that is to say His carrying out Holiness in His domain, is done in Heaven, we accept the responsibility for carrying out that Holy Will in the domain He has given us to manage. This is not about what God will do as much as it is about what He has given us to do. We are His stewards. A steward is responsible for carrying out the values and directives of His master, independently of the steward's personal interests or concerns. Most prayers focus on the personal concerns of those who are praying. *God is not the steward of our values and wishes; we are the stewards of His!* Yet people generally pray as though God is our on-call errand boy. God is not a valet. It is no wonder so few prayers are answered. They fail to take into consideration God's prime directive: that we are obliged to be His agents of holiness in the world. A prayer that fails to acknowledge our basic stewardship responsibility to God's holiness directive is a prayer of vanity, if not blasphemy.

3. God's Provision—"Give us this day our daily bread"

As we depend on God for moral direction, we depend on Him to provide us with the physical strength we need to carry out our moral stewardship. Evil will attempt to extort us into forsaking holiness by denying us jobs and money and, therefore, food and shelter. Moral compromise in order to maintain a job is like Esau's selling his birthright for oatmeal.[85] It is not a good bargain. When evil people deny us these things, we ask God to supply them. It is not just because we need food to live. God knows that. We need to live in order to be advocates for the holiness God expects. Recall Elijah.[86] When pursued by the evil Jezebel, he fled for his life and found the gracious widow whose faith was rewarded with oil and grain that never ran out. Elijah lives to become God's advocate against the forces of institutionalized evil. So too must we. Pray for daily food for the daily job, for being advocates for what is true, right, and good.

---

85 Genesis 25:19 ff

86 I Kings 18

4. God's Grace—"Forgive us our trespasses as we forgive those who have trespassed against us"

There is a basic principle of reciprocity here. There is a basic moral condition attached to receiving God's forgiveness. To be forgiven, one must forgive "as God has forgiven." Recall that our fourth principle of holiness requires that every person be responsible for being proactive in the reconciliation of everyone to God and to each other. *Forgiveness is not unconditional!* God's forgiving anyone rests on his/her accepting responsibility for holiness in him/herself and others. The forgiveness twaddle of our present age consists in tolerance without accountability. This is a license for licentiousness. Obviously, not even an omnipotent holy God can permit such a thing without compromising holiness itself. Holiness can never be sacrificed on the altar of tolerance. Repentance is the condition of forgiveness; therefore, forgiving others means working for people's repentance as well as working on our own. God forgives our sin in virtue of our working on repentance. We forgive others in virtue of their working on their repentance. What we can never do is to be intolerant of those who accept the responsibility for becoming as holy as God expects. This kind of intolerance violates God's holiness.

The objective of moral imperatives is less about making people pay than it is about helping them to accept the responsibility for repenting. In saying "forgive us our debts as we forgive those of others," we acknowledge that anyone who experiences God's grace must accept responsibility for becoming as holy as God expects. We are qualitatively no different in this regard than any other human being who has lived, is living, or ever will live. The moral imperative is to use forgiveness as a carrot for a commitment to make positive moral changes.

There is a potential for some misunderstanding here. It could be interpreted that these comments imply that it is appropriate to be unforgiving until people accept responsibility for their sins. This is absolutely the wrong course to take. The four Kingdom values control how the Kingdom disciple relates to sinners. The disciple views other people as people who have yet to repent. A disciple of the Kingdom is not permitted to take on the position of God in judging people. Final judgment is reserved for God after He has determined that there is no more justification for allowing people to exercise their free will in the interest of evil. The Kingdom disciple takes the position of Christ who sees some sinners as those who are sick and in need of a physician. Christ associates with sinners in order to influence them to repent, as principle 2 requires. As Jesus says in His defense, "I have come not to call the righteous but sinners to repentance."[87] The Kingdom disciple also takes the position of Christ with regard to arrogant sinners. As Christ would confront the sin of the scribes and Pharisees, so the Kingdom disciple will not shrink from acting as a prophet, the critic of sin and sinning.

5. God's Attendance—"Lead us not into temptation, but deliver us from evil."

The one thing that assures anyone of moral purity and holiness is knowing that God's holiness and following His moral directives will never lead one toward evil. The prayer then is for God to stay close so that He may remind us in times of temptation that He believes in His servants. Temptation diminishes the more surpassingly righteous we become.

If being heard speaking pious words is the objective and if being heard doing so is important to someone's self-esteem, then that objective will be satisfied. And whatever reward one seeks in this way is all the reward available. But for those who care passionately about coming to the full measure of the stature of Christ, such practices are shallow twaddle. Those who want to become as holy as God justifiably expects will not care that no one may hear what they pray. At least, in this case, should they be overheard, someone will overhear someone being honest.

Fasting—A Discipline of Self-control

I will not discuss fasting as a practice. It has spiritual value, to be sure. It is even important to undergo fasts from time to time in order to develop the disciplines of the faith. But Jesus's major point here is not about whether or not to fast. In this case, as in the others, He takes it for granted that people will do so. He takes it for granted that spiritual people will fast, as they also give alms and pray. Rather the issue is the motivation and intention of the person who does these things.

Which is the more moral, the more holy—to appear righteous or to be righteous? The answer is morally clear. Someone who merely presents a righteous appearance is never as holy as someone who is righteous as a matter of character. Think about a performer, especially a professional one. Advertising firms use something called a testimonial. They employ famous people to pitch some product or service. These people may be athletes or

---

87 Matthew 9:13, Mark 2:17, Luke 5:32

other celebrities. But they also employ the services of actors or entertainers. These actors may or may not be celebrities. The actor or entertainer is a professional at portraying characters that are not his/her own. The better the actor, the greater the divergence there can be between who they are as a person and the parts they can play. Yet a genuine testimonial has value solely in virtue of the genuineness of the testimony. The one who testifies as to the quality of the product should be genuine in the testimony. But, by definition, an actor has the professional talent to hide the real person behind the public persona. It is called "putting on an act." Therefore, the testimonial is compromised by the fact that, given the behavior, there is no way, based on the performance alone, to assess the quality of the testimonial. *Even should the testimonial be genuine, those who have to rely on it cannot rely on it.*

There is a preacher in a regional Bible college who is widely acknowledged as a "powerful preacher." It is absolutely given that he will cry at some point in every one of his sermons. We who have been observing his style for over twenty-five years have become a bit cynical of his crying. The more he does it, the more its genuineness suffers. Anyone whose emotional presentation can respond to a line in his sermon notes prompting him to "cry here" presents a dubious performance. Things that are contrived for effect on an audience may be harmless enough in a movie or stage play, but when a talent like this is devoted to manipulating political or religious belief, it is no more than an alternative way of selling snake oil. Genuineness is something that does not have to be contrived for public consumption. Someone who is genuine does not contrive a presentation. Rather, she/he will never even think about an action in terms of its perception. To do so taints the action itself.

This phenomenon worries me most about the emphasis on praise and worship in contemporary Christianity. When one organizes worship to create an emotional response and the performers become skilled in the performance arts and the performance is enhanced by means of lighting and sound controls, the worship itself is violated since worship itself is the spontaneous expression of genuine love and allegiance. Somehow I think that the worship of Christians in Rome's catacombs was more genuine than worship that depends on thousands of dollars' worth of high-tech equipment and intense mandatory rehearsals. Worship is not a stage play, neither is it a Las Vegas or Branson show. Worship leaders and preachers are not performance artists, or at least, to the extent that they are the worship they manipulate becomes disingenuous. The congregation is not an audience to be entertained so that attendance can be stabilized at continuingly higher levels, the assertions of worship leaders and ministers of music to the contrary notwithstanding.

Hiding an Action

A perceptive student will ask for an important clarification. Recall that Jesus had said earlier that a disciple will "let his/her good works shine before men so that they may glorify the Father who is in Heaven." Can someone say that the practices of almsgiving, praying, and fasting are merely ways in which people display their good works for the praise of God? If they are, then this admonition is at least confusing if not outright contradictory. Are good works to be public or private? Are the expressions of our spirituality to be public or private? The way to address this problem is to realize that Jesus is always concerned about genuineness and never about performance.

CHAPTER 11—WEALTH & WORRY: MATTHEW 6:19–34

Previously, Jesus had focused on things people should do with the precaution that they should not do them for the plaudits of people. The motivations or intentions people bring to any ethical activity are morally important. Two people performing the same moral activity with the only difference between them is that one does it for the praise of someone and the other does it for the sake of the good in itself do not enjoy the same moral status with regard to those actions. Clearly, the morally superior person is the one who does a good act for the act's own sake and not in the hope of receiving praise or avoiding blame. Jesus now turns His attention to acts that ought to be stopped. The translation of the following three examples fails to adequately represent the words in the original language. There are two ways of prohibiting something in Greek. First, a prohibition may take the form of not beginning to do something. This form of prohibition presumes that some action is contemplated but not yet undertaken. The second form of the prohibition is to stop some action that has begun. Although the translations of this section present the former interpretation, the Greek construction is of the latter kind. What Jesus says is designed to get people to *stop* treasuring, worrying, and judging. Jesus wants the priorities to be right.

I doubt that these examples are exhaustive. There may be other priority issues people have to morally face, but these are clearly the most prevalent ones. The first two have to do with perspectives on wealth. The last has to do with relating to people. These temptations have the potential for tainting every action and the development of every moral character.

WORRY, WEALTH, AND THE LOGIC OF ACQUISITION

There is perhaps no greater threat to the development of moral character than the issue of wealth, whether having too little or too much. Either we want to acquire as much as possible (Jesus calls this "treasuring"), or we have little of it and worry about not having it. It seems that everything we need needs to be purchased. We need food, clothing, shelter, and perhaps transportation and toys. The myth of wealth is that the finer these things can be, the better we can live. This is the logic of acquisition. From wealth we can derive power, prestige, property, and pleasure. The more wealth we have, the more and the better of these things we can have. On the other side, when we lack enough of property, pleasure, power, and prestige, we worry about getting enough of them. Worry easily adopts the logic of acquisition.

The Great Depression of the 1930s provides a wonderfully clear lesson on this logic of acquisition. During this economic crisis, many people became unemployed. Some people who were formerly wealthy were rudely introduced to poverty. Some saw nothing more to live for. Poverty was intolerable. Not having what they considered the requisite amount of power, prestige, property, or pleasure meant that life was no longer worth living. Many suicides occurred in the midst of this economic crisis. This fact reveals the logic of acquisition. "Who I am is a function of what I have."

The logic of acquisition also shows itself in Depression survivors. It created a kind of hoarding mentality. Those who were children and had to grow up in this period became adults with a worry that they should be prepared against anything like this occurring again. It is not that they thought that they could prevent a national catastrophe but that they themselves would make sure that they had adequate provisions should it occur again. People learned how to grow food in gardens, to can, freeze and store the food. People were judicious in making sure that their money was never spent frivolously. People made their own clothes; younger children wore the clothes of their elder siblings. Families with older children lent or gave their children's clothes to the younger children of their friends and neighbors. People rarely bought new things. As long as things still worked, there was no justification for buying something new. When these people did buy something, they paid cash for it, whether it was a new car or a piece of farm equipment. Their value was that if you did not have the money to pay for it, you couldn't afford it. As a result, these families had increasingly large caches of cash and commodities. Looking at their outward appearances, one would think that they had little or nothing in terms of hard assets, yet they became quite wealthy. They worried in order not to worry.

The logic of acquisition was also apparent in the moral crisis created by the forty-second president of the United States. Although his sexual indiscretions, his lying under oath, and obstruction of justice were criticized by nearly everyone, they were generally excused on the ground that to change presidents would jeopardize the good economy. According to the polls, people had considered the question of whether sexual indiscretion was more or less important than economic well-being and answered that question by saying that wealth acquisition and preservation is the more important value. Economic well-being trumps any moral turpitude.

While worry because of poverty may focus on what one does not have, it also focuses on wealth acquisition. Both suffer from the Jacob/Esau syndrome.[88] Jacob's conniving greed meets Esau's shortsighted hunger. Jacob will take any opportunity to acquire what is not his. Esau is willing to sell something precious in order to acquire short-term gratification.

I once was lecturing to my college ethics class on this matter. We were discussing what a lab technician's moral responsibility was if he was engaged in running blood tests on African American males during the Tuskegee syphilis study.[89] African American males in Macon County, Alabama, who had contracted syphilis were studied but not treated in order to study the effects of the disease on them. They were not told that they had syphilis, but that they had "bad blood." If the lab tech should expose the practice of studying but not treating these men, he risks losing his job and, therefore, jeopardizing his family's economic well-being. If he ignores the moral issues surrounding the project, he may secure his job, but at what moral costs? One student signaled his value system and reflected the dominant view on this matter. He said that a person's first allegiance was to the person that "cut the check." The student who made this remark was, incidentally, African American.[90]

---

88 Genesis 27

89 For the "Report of the Tuskegee Syphilis Study Legacy Committee" May 20, 1996 as well as a bibliography of works on the Tuskegee Syphilis Study see: www.med.virginia.edu/hs-library/historical/apology/report.html.

90 Another of my African-American inmate students argues quite frequently that arresting and incarcerating people, particularly blacks, for trafficking in drugs is the

One can see the right moral thing to do by altering the circumstances. Consider not that you are the lab tech but that you are one of the men on whom the study was being conducted. Would you want someone in the position of the lab technician to become your advocate or ignore the morality issues to assure his own financial condition or career track and blow the whistle on this morally outrageous policy? Would the conclusion to preserve the income from employment be acceptable if one of your loved ones were among the guinea pigs? The answer becomes clearer once one changes the perspective of the characters. Clearly, the different moral perspectives are not morally equivalent.

This is the moral problem with the acquisition of wealth. Once one makes the decision to acquire wealth, the die is cast. Every subsequent decision is made with a view to how that decision affects the objective of economic well-being. It matters little whether the moral decision to accumulate wealth consists in getting a little more or a lot more. The morality is the same. One has traded the well-being of self and others for some combination of property, pleasure, prestige, or power. One has said in setting priorities and values that any and all people are useful insofar as they contribute to the objective of getting one or more of the four Ps.

Jesus argues that this immorality will not stand in the Kingdom of God. Jesus argues that it is foolish for someone to strive to continually acquire things that waste away or that other corrupt people covet as much as they do. One steals from people who have more than she/he does. One steals from people who have what she/he does not have. Karl Marx[91] had at least one thing right. Greed justifies exploitation. Exploitation breeds alienation. Alienation culminates in hostility. Jesus will tolerate none of this justification logic. The disciple of the Kingdom of God will surpass this greed by realizing that people have more value than things. Jesus requires that His disciples realize that the value of things always depreciates, while

---

equivalent of arresting and incarcerating any businessman. He does not come to the suburbs to carry on his business, and he is merely providing a service to people who choose to buy his product. This is not an "African-American" logic. It is an application of the logic of acquisition.

91   For a sense of Marx's moral outrage at the exploitative practices of British Capitalism of the 19th century, see Marx's *Economic and Philosophic Manuscripts* as well as that of his colleague Frederick Engels *The Condition of the Working Class in England in 1844.*

the value of people always appreciates.[92] No Kingdom disciple will ever trade his/her integrity for prestige, property, power, or pleasure.[93]

WORRY AND WEALTH

Listening to sermonic discourses on worrying, one would think that the concern has little to do with wealth or poverty, yet Jesus frames this portion of His *Sermon* in terms of "treasuring" and "worrying" about the provisions of life. His conclusion is that

> No one can serve two masters. Either he will hate the one and love the other, or he will be devoted to the one and despise the other. You cannot serve both God and money.[94]

Acquisition is one focus of worrying. It is the same phenomenon whether one has much and wants more, or one has little and wants more. We have all been around people who worry about things. Most wealthy people or people working on becoming wealthy worry incessantly. Their worry has little to do with becoming as holy as God justifiably expects and much to do with spending as much time and energy in acquiring things that become obsolete. Jesus asks a very intelligent question, as He often does. "Why would anyone spend time and energy focusing on the acquisition of stuff that only deteriorates? What sense does it make to spend time and energy on making stuff for others to acquire when that stuff will only depreciate as soon as it moves from the store to the car?" Even the car itself is worth less the moment it is driven off the lot. The minute a company designs a new product, the R&D people have to begin to surpass the product they have just released. Most often, this drive to create new depreciating stuff is due to the fact that others will find a way to legally or illegally steal the stuff; so designers, engineers, and executives continue the endless cycle of

---

92 Matthew 6:19

93 A poignant contrast is formed by understanding that Charles Dickens writes his *A Christmas Carol* during the same period that Marx and Engels were writing their revolutionary econo-philosophy. Dickens takes the approach of the Christianity of the New Testament as the real solution to the social evils of this period. Scrooge comes to comprehend the meaning of Christmas in terms of meeting human needs and repentance of his greed.

94 Matthew 6:24

worry about and work of foiling thieves. They either try making their stuff unstealable or continually create new stuff with the full acknowledgment that someone will steal it. So to stay ahead of the thieves, they must keep creating more and more stealable stuff.

Consider how Jesus argues His point about worry. The first observation is that Jesus says, "Because of this I say to you, 'Stop worrying'." The examples all have to do with life provision.[95] God knows that food, housing, and health are important. "Stop worrying about what to wear or what to eat." It is as though Jesus understands that people absorbed in poverty have to worry about how to get the meager but necessary things. "Is not life worth more than clothing?" One needs very little to survive, if survival is the objective. But it is not worth surviving if surviving means selling one's integrity as Esau sold his birthright for oatmeal.

"SEEKING THE KINGDOM OF HEAVEN AND ITS RIGHTEOUSNESS FIRST"

Jesus seems to realize how strong the instinct of self-preservation is in us. But the test of moral courage is to be able to will to do what is good when our instincts seem to compel us to do what is immoral. This differentiates human beings in the image of God and animals. Instinct is the final reality in an animal, but with man, it is different. God has imbued us with a will. It must serve the interest of determining what actions ought to be willed.

Immanuel Kant criticized the ethics of David Hume by making this point. Hume had argued that morality depends solely on what he called "sensation." He further argued that it could not depend on Reason, but rather that Reason is the servant of the appetites. In other words, Hume believed that Reason was called to serve the interest of the appetites. For him, Reason could not decide whether a given appetite ought to be served. However, after an appetite had come to the fore, Reason was used to decide what strategies would satisfy the appetite.

If Hume were right about this, the whole notion of moral responsibility could no longer survive. One could only be responsible for whatever strategy she/he used in satisfying the instinct or appetite, not for the instinct or appetite itself. Once someone is hungry, Reason cannot decide whether the hunger ought to be satisfied. That is not negotiable. The appetite is

---

95 Matthew 6:25

compelling. Reason must serve the hunger and decide how to satisfy it, so Reason would investigate whether buying food or stealing food was the more efficient means of satisfying the hunger. If one hasn't the money to buy the food, then Reason determines whether working or stealing is the way to satisfy hunger. If it decides that stealing is the way to acquire it, Reason then begins its work on the strategy for stealing it. Should one steal it openly, or surreptitiously? Does one "borrow" the food with no intention of replacing it, or does one sneak into a store or a house to steal it? Perhaps it is better not to steal the food itself since it would be cumbersome and noisy to fill paper bags with food, so stealing the money for the food is better. One is particularly justified in stealing from people who have a surplus of the things I need. These people are greedy, and stealing from greedy people is morally justified. It matters not whether the stealing is direct as breaking into a house or a store or stealing by committing fraud against an insurance company or taking it in the form of taxes that provide subsidies. One may not have the luxury of time to steal in this way since bureaucracies are so slow. It is, however, very efficient to steal by stealing a credit card or creating a fraudulent credit card. Then the credit card company can pay rather than victimize some real person. This same process occurs when anyone has any appetite whatsoever.

Kant argued that this analysis left out of consideration something he called the Good Will. The Good Will leaves room for something one could call the Bad Will. Kant thought that the Will could become good when one chooses to analyze every action in terms of what he called the Categorical Imperative. For Kant, Reason serves the Will. One must engage Reason in deciding whether it is good or not to satisfy some appetite. The Categorical Imperative says: "One is morally obligated to act in such a way that she/he could will without contradiction that his/her action becomes a universal moral obligation."

My daughter majored in philosophy at Illinois Wesleyan University, and in one of her ethics classes, she had to write a paper on the question whether Kant's Categorical Imperative was the Golden Rule dressed in philosophical garb. I will not argue this question. I will observe that in philosophy departments, the question of the standard of universalizing an action as a moral test is worthy of consideration. In my own ethics classes, I put forward as a universal test something akin to Jesus's formulation of the Golden Rule.[96] The Golden Rule Test says, "If someone knows when

---

96 Matthew 7:12

she/he is being treated unjustly, then that person knows what it is to treat others unjustly." The consequence of this when applying Kant's Categorical Imperative is that any failure or refusal to consider the universality of one's actions is to violate one's moral duty. To steal is to authorize being stolen from on the ground that "one is morally obligated to act in such a way that she/he could will without contradiction that his/her action becomes a universal moral obligation."[97] On the contrary, one is never morally permitted to act contrary to what one expects of others.

So Jesus expects of those who would become His disciples to put primary things before secondary things. The primary things are 1) that people deserve to be treated with dignity and respect, 2) that everyone is responsible for holiness in oneself and others, 3) that everyone is responsible for being an advocate for what is true, right, and good, and 4) that everyone is responsible for being proactive in the reconciliation of all people to each other and to God. One can either strive for the acquisition of wealth or worry at not having it, or one can live for the fulfillment of the law in seeking the Kingdom of God first. There is no middle ground. Jesus says: "No one can serve two masters. Either he will hate the one and love the other, or he will be devoted to the one and despise the other. You cannot serve both God and money."[98]

---

97 Kant argues this point thusly, "Another finds himself forced by necessity to borrow money. He knows that he will not be able to repay it, but sees also that nothing will be lent to him unless he promises stoutly to repay it in a definite time. He desires to make this promise, but he has still so much conscience as to ask himself: "Is it not unlawful and inconsistent with duty to get out of a difficulty in this way?" Suppose however that he resolves to do so: then the maxim of his action would be expressed thus: "When I think myself in want of money, I will borrow money and promise to repay it, although I know that I never can do so." Now this principle of self-love or of one's own advantage may perhaps be consistent with my whole future welfare; but the question now is, "Is it right?" I change the suggestion of self-love into a universal law, and state the question thus: "How would it be if my maxim were a universal law?" Then I see at once that it could never hold as a universal law of nature, but would necessarily contradict itself. For supposing it to be a universal law that everyone when he thinks himself in a difficulty would be able to promise whatever he pleases, with the purpose of not keeping his promise, the promise itself would become impossible, as well as the end that one might have in view in it, since no one would consider that anything was promised to him, but would ridicule all such statements as vain pretences [sic]." *Fundamental Principles of the Metaphysic of Morals* Second Section

98 Matthew 6:24

CHAPTER 12—"Judge Not . . ." is not what it appears: Matthew 7:1–27

If I could, I would wave a magic wand and change a really silly belief. It is the belief that passing moral judgment is morally wrong. It is a belief of many Christians and most non-Christians, and especially the Christophobic. First of all, there are people who pontificate that Christians who condemn immorality violate their own standards. Secondly, people advocate the moral principle of nonjudgmentality on the ground that anyone who passes moral judgment does so illegitimately unless she/he is morally untainted, and since it is not possible for this to be true (no one is, after all, perfect), anyone who does so is a hypocrite. Third, it is a higher moral principle to forgive than to judge.

I have never been able to figure out how people could argue this way without being embarrassed at the inconsistencies, even the irrationality of their arguments. If it is necessarily true, that is to say that it is universally true, to say of moral judgment that anyone who passes moral judgment must be morally untainted, why does anyone think that passing moral judgment on people who think passing moral judgment is a moral obligation is behaving immorally?

This summarizes the doctrine of moral relativism:

1. *All* moral values and therefore *all* moral judgments are merely personal points of view.
2. *No one* has the moral right to pass moral judgment on or impose a merely personal moral belief on another.

These two beliefs appeal to a universal moral principle, not merely a personal one (i.e., no one has the right to impose a personal moral value on another). Those who hold these or similar beliefs argue not just to state a personal belief but to compel, either by argument or by other forms of pressure, that others are somehow obligated to adopt their relativistic point of view, either as a rational or a moral principle.

The doctrine of moral relativism is widespread. It is uncritically accepted and promulgated. The easiest way to show its intellectual bankruptcy is to expose that fact that in stating the doctrine of moral relativism, one is logically compelled to appeal to some moral universal. If there are no moral universals, it seems it would be difficult to appeal to one. If there is at least one moral universal, then moral relativism is false. The instant anyone is logically forced to appeal to a doctrine that moral relativists argue is false, that argument is vitiated.

The most common form of this fallacy is the claim that "Anyone can do anything she/he wishes to do, as long as it doesn't hurt anybody." Let's say that I want to choose a personal morality that frees me to inflict pain as a source of my pleasure or happiness. Am I free to do so? Well, if it is true that *all* moral values are personal, it seems that I am free to do so. With this result, I am completely content. No one can interfere with me in the pursuits of my personal values. But now I am confronted with the *as-long-as* condition. Now, as a moral relativist, I have no problem with someone who has a personal moral value system that does not include using the pain of others as a source of personal satisfaction. Others can, after all, live however they choose. They may even change their personal value systems as often or as arbitrarily as they may wish, just as I may. But this is not the status of the *as-long-as* condition. The *as-long-as* condition does not say that one can adopt the personal moral principle: "*I* can do anything *I* wish as long as *I* don't hurt anyone, and others may or may not adopt this principle as they choose." Rather, the *as-long-as* condition says something entirely different and incompatible with moral relativism. The *as-long-as* condition puts a restriction on the choices a person may adopt as a personal moral value system. Therefore, it violates the doctrine of moral relativity. If there is an *as-long-as* condition, then there is at least one moral universal. If there is at least one moral universal, then it cannot be true to say that there are no moral universals that apply to all people at all times and in all places. So it would seem that some form of moral universalism is true, even if the *as-long-as* condition were the only form.

Once the door to some form of moral universalism is open, there is now no *a priori* reason to restrict the number of moral universals to this particular one. Surely, there may be more of them. If there are more of them, or could be more of them, we should look for them. We should listen to the proposals and arguments for or against other candidates for moral universals. We can study those presented in the Scriptures for the qualities and characteristics they embody and use them in establishing the adequacy of any other proposed moral principles. We should have some way of deciding between competing versions of them.

If it is possible that moral universals exist, then we have to investigate whether it is legitimate for someone to appeal to them in making moral judgments. Either it is true to say that people who violate some or even many moral principles may cast moral judgments, or it is true to say that such people cannot. If we take the latter option, that no one is permitted to make moral judgments if she/he has ever violated the moral principle that is the basis of that moral judgment, the moral voice in society would be muted. The consequences of such a social policy are devastating. A society with no moral voice will be left vulnerable to the whims of anyone's personal morality. This may be desirable as a strategy to allow people to avoid embarrassment. But it can do nothing to reduce or eliminate injustice.

When I worked in the environment of the Department of Corrections, I was required to attend a training session. At this session, this conflict between moral universalism and moral relativism came to a head. The Department of Corrections incarcerates people who have been convicted of violating the law. Presumably, convictions for things like murder, manslaughter, burglary, robbery, embezzlement, assault (sexual and otherwise), extortion, and so on are not merely violations of law. Presumably, these things are violations of law because they violate the moral principles a society requires in order to function with some modicum of social cohesion. No one in this training ever acted as though inmates had a right (a right derived from whence I have no idea since moral relativism is said to be true) to adopt and live by whatever moral values that they themselves may choose. Throughout the training, we were warned of the deviancy and malice of those people we have to work with and around every day. Our safety and the "security of the institution" depended on our taking precautions against being manipulated by these people. Even their most innocent remarks or behaviors will more than likely have some malicious intent. Why, if all morals are personal and immune from the judgment of others, is it proper for us to have prisons at all?

This issue came up in the obligatory discussion of inmate rights and cultural diversity. Some person who was mentally awake during this discussion asked why some people were incarcerated for following what their culture permitted or advocated. Urban inner-city culture is not the same as the culture of the suburbs and even more different from rural culture. So what right do suburban-rural people have to impose their values on people of inner-city culture? The cultural diversity consciousness of our present time is merely an extension of the principle of moral relativism. No one may judge the actions of people within another culture. Does the Department of Corrections incarcerate people who are merely following their personal or cultural values? The relativist answer is yes, but that answer apparently does not undercut the moral propriety of imprisoning people whose actions have violated just laws. This means that the principle of moral relativism is nonsense, just as is the principle that no person who has violated a moral principle is forever excluded from making a moral judgment is nonsense. If such relativistic notions are correct, no one who is in prison is there justly since everyone there is there by following his/her own personal value system. Further, no one has the moral right to deny others of their right to choose their personal values. Moral relativism is either idiocy or chaos.

One view takes it for granted that when Jesus says, "Judge not that you be not judged, for the judgment you use will be used with you" that it is proper to say that if people do not judge others, then God will not judge them. The other view is that since God readily forgives people, He does not cast moral judgments about what people do. Both of these interpretations are just wrong. The first case is wrong because it requires that it is true that God makes His decision about our status based on how we judge others. The implication is that when we are intolerant towards others, God will be intolerant towards us, and He will be tolerant towards us when we are tolerant towards others. It presumes that if we tolerate the immorality of others, that God will tolerate our immorality. But why should anyone suppose that God would tolerate any immorality at all? If He does, He becomes unjust; and if He does not, this reasoning crumbles. The second view is that "God readily forgives people" means the same thing as "God does not cast moral judgments." To see that this is not true, one only has to conceive of some circumstance in which it would be true to say "God readily forgives" but would not say "God does not cast moral judgments." This is very easy to do. The very notion of "forgiveness" means that someone has violated a moral principle and that another person will not, under the most liberal interpretation of "forgiveness," hold that person accountable for that moral turpitude. This means that the one who forgives has passed a moral judgment—not that he has not or refuses to. For God to refuse to cast a moral judgment means that God either has no moral standards or He refuses to hold Himself or anyone else to those standards. In this case, it is hardly relevant to say that God is holy or just or righteous. If this is true, then the whole tone of the *Sermon* is vitiated. Jesus requires that we use the principle of moral discrimination first in removing the log from our own eyes before we set about removing the specks from the eyes of others. This does not eliminate moral discrimination; it raises it to a higher moral plane.

If it is true that people who have violated a moral principle may make moral judgments, or are morally obligated to make moral judgments, then there is a moral voice in an immoral wilderness. There is also a voice for accepting the responsibility for repentance. There is moral virtue in someone's being able to say that she/he has violated some moral universal and experiences remorse for it and now repudiates doing it again. Such moral confession is more than merely saying, "I have violated my own moral principle."

Finally, we should use moral universals in discriminating between people and their use or abuse of them. Let's say that there are moral universals, but no one is ever justified in using them as guides in assessing the conduct of others. Let us further say that even should anyone violate some moral universal, it should never be used to judge him/her. Presumably, people who would argue this way will have to say that this is another moral universal—namely that it is universally immoral for anyone to make a moral judgment on another person. But if this is true, what then is the status of the moral universal that no one should make a moral judgment on another? It must be that it is immoral to adopt it as a moral universal, or else it is moral to do so. In the former case, we have a contradiction namely that one must both adopt and not adopt this moral universal. In the latter case, if it is moral to adopt a moral universal, we have the same contradiction. Surely there is a problem with a belief that requires us to maintain one contradiction—but two?

Shallow thinkers notwithstanding, Jesus does not and would never advocate or argue for such twaddle. Jesus has just advocated the moral standard that people who will enter God's Kingdom must have a surpassing righteousness. He says that they must be the salt of the earth and the light of the world. He sets a standard of holiness that requires people to be more than just holy in action. He requires that their holy action be grounded in holy character. He exposes the hypocrisy of people whose only motivation for doing good actions is having people praise them. His closing illustration distinguishes between wise and foolish people. And yet, in the middle of this profound moral discourse, people will argue that Jesus sets forth a doctrine that advocates that people are morally obligated to withhold moral judgment. Now if I were convinced that this is what Jesus has done, I could find little to praise. A blunder so massive would deserve not praise, but derision. Such a level of intellectual inconsistency would deserve relegating this man to wearing a dunce cap and sitting him in the corner of the room. No other member of the class should ever be allowed to think that this type of argument is worthy of anything but contempt.

The standard of surpassing righteousness requires, in addition to personal moral character, the ability to discern between the appearances of moral character and moral character itself. The first and foremost standard of surpassing righteousness is that the Kingdom disciple has the personal integrity to live by the moral universal she/he advocates. No one should ever labor under the nonsensical illusion that God is morally indifferent. Everyone who would be a Kingdom disciple must understand that in casting a legitimate moral judgment, she/he places him/herself under the aegis of the moral principle underlying that moral judgment. She/he need not think that God will use any other moral standard than the one we ourselves are willing to use in the defense of our own interest in justice. Jesus introduces the so-called "Golden Rule" here. Everyone is morally obligated to treat other people in exactly the same way that she/he expects to be treated. It is a foregone conclusion that no person will remain silent when being dealt with unjustly. Any demeaning of our dignity—any person who is indifferent to our well-being, safety, or dignity violates his/her moral obligation to me. In my ethics classes, I advocate at least one test for the fact that all people know the moral universals and expect other people to know them and act consistently with them. It is the "Golden Rule Test" which says, "If I know what it is to be treated unjustly, then I know what it is to treat others unjustly." Therefore, I am morally obligated to every other person in the universe to treat them in exactly the same way I expect them to treat me, whether I am treated that way or not. The illustrations that follow the principle of "judge not that you be not judged" reveals not that passing moral judgment is morally improper but that it is most powerful when exercised by people who have "removed the log from their own eye."

But it is not enough to merely exercise personal integrity in making moral judgments. One must be an advocate for what is true, right, and good. One must, in dealing with others, distinguish between true and false prophets, dogs and swine, wolves in sheep's clothing. The Kingdom disciple is responsible for discernment in listening to and accepting or rejecting what she/he hears and sees. This warning about judging is as much about being careful in exercising discernment as it is about personal integrity.

CHAPTER 13—AND THEY WERE AMAZED!
MATTHEW 7:28

There are two kinds of authority. There is formal authority and moral authority. Although most of us recognize the difference, we still act confused. We long for those who have formal authority to have moral authority as well. Formal authority consists in someone's occupying some official position or office. People who have formal authority are also given the power to enforce compliance with that authority. They often give that authority to themselves through legislation. Political office holders have some kind of policing authority. It is no accident that the term "police" and "politics" have similar spellings. The Law they administer as well as the agency used to enforce it is external. It is something that must be imposed from outside. It is alien.

There is no necessary correlation between having formal authority and having moral authority. The law does not define what is true, right, or good. Rather what is true, right, and good defines the difference between just and unjust laws. If Law identified what is true, right, and good then no unjust law could exist. What was moral would be just what the law said it was. It is so obviously untrue to say such a thing that it is hardly worth laboring the point. There are unjust laws as there are unjust men.

THE "KISS" PRINCIPLE IS THE KISS OF DEATH.

Plato's *Republic* presented a paradigm that has come to control much of the way people look at leadership and authority. Plato argued that society should be organized with the Philosopher-King at the top of a societal pyramid. The Philosopher-King had both wisdom and authority. His pronouncements were to be followed since he was both wise and just. Others in society had the responsibility for following this wise and just leader. The Guardians guaranteed compliance with the directives of the Philosopher-King. The artisans and the masses, not being nearly as wise as the Philosopher-King, had to be compelled to comply when they were unwilling to do so. They were in effect too dumb and too compromised by other loyalties, like friendship and family, to be trusted with anything as potentially treacherous as self-determination. The *hoi polloi* are people who need to be taken care of and who must be compelled to do things that they would not naturally do owing to their ignorance relative to the Philosopher-King.

It worries me that Christianity has followed this platonic model of leadership.[99] Throughout the centuries, even the millennia, since the church first began, that priests and clergy function as the Philosopher-Kings and Guardians of "the Faith." Popes and archbishops and bishops and clergy of all kinds have perpetrated all kinds of blasphemous evil in the name of Christ primarily because of the arrogance of power and the belief that the masses are too stupid or too depraved to be treated with high moral expectations. After all, as long as one's salvation depends on what the clergy says, people who are not as learned will have to depend on their blessing.

The original motivation of the Protestant Reformation was to correct the excesses of Platonic leadership model in the church. Luther, for example, translated the Bible into the vernacular of the people in order to wrest intellectual control for salvation from the papacy and give it to the people. As admirable as this was, it fell short of what Jesus expects due to the fact that the Reformers retained the Catholic doctrine of original sin in the form of the doctrine of the total depravity of man. If people are too stupid or too depraved to understand, much less comply with holiness, then their salvation depends on the dispensation of God's grace by God's agents—the priests or clergy. Luther was, after all, a very brilliant monk.

The KISS principle perpetuates mediocrity. The KISS principle argues that in order to "sell" anything one must "Keep It Simple, Stupid!" For every doctrine, idea, or concept no "ordinary Christian" will pay attention unless the message comes to him/her in a simple form, the simpler the better. Sermons, Sunday school lessons, and Bible study formats are presented in

---

99   For a profound analysis and critique of Plato's political philosophy see Karl R Popper *The Open Society and Its Enemies* 2 Volumes [Princeton, NJ: Princeton University Press, 1971]

an "edutainment" [educational entertainment] format. In a church I used to attend, the adult Christian education director once selected a study book for a summer adult small-group program. One of my friends asked me to look at the study book and disclose what I thought of it. My comment was to ask whether crayons came with the book. The book was insulting to the intelligence of any self-respecting adult. It was patronizing, paternalistic, and demeaning. Not only would I have been insulted that this "minister" would select such a "study" book. I could not imagine that any publishing house, much less a reputable one, would deign to consider publishing it. Yet it is more likely that a study book that challenges a disciple to think and reason and genuinely study difficult doctrines and complex problems of morality and faith will get more rejection letters than will these children's books for adults. This is due to the fact that even the publishers believe that people are either too stupid or too bored by such an approach. The objective is, after all, to sell books—not to make disciples. "Keeping it simple" guarantees that the church will be populated with people who are increasingly dumbed down to a despicable ignorance and a correspondingly inadequate capacity to witness effectively to anyone. "Keeping it simple" guarantees that churches will be populated with simple, stupid people—at least in spiritual matters.

Dr. Charles Spurgeon was often criticized for preaching sermons that "went over the people's heads." Dr. Spurgeon consistently responded, "Well then, let them lift up their heads." Is this response harsh and insensitive? Unfortunately, many would say that it is. Yet Dr. Spurgeon understood something we have yet to comprehend. People will rise only to the level of their leader's expectations. Setting mediocre discipleship expectations guarantees spiritual mediocrity as much as it provides job security. Those who would demand or even respond to challenging discipleship will hardly be a sufficiently large majority to counterbalance those who are willing to accept lesser challenges. This is no doubt why Jesus says that many people will pass through the wide gate over the broad road leading to destruction while only a few will travel the narrow way through the strait gate. I seriously doubt that any interpretation of the *Sermon* or of the Great Commission would justify these expectations of mediocrity. There is nothing of mediocrity in the *Sermon*! No one who has expectations of mediocrity will ever teach or lead with the moral authority that amazed those who heard Jesus speak!

"EARNESTLY DESIRE THE HIGHEST GIFTS, ESPECIALLY THAT YOU PROPHESY."

I think it is no accident that Jesus held no office of official authority. In fact, the apostle John, in his gospel, identifies Jesus as *"the* Prophet." Prophets were the moral conscience of Israel and Judah. They came from all strata of society and from both genders. Often they had no particular societally recognized position of power. Therefore, the power of their message could only be moral. Although Jesus takes on the mantle of the high priest in the Hebrew Epistle, He was not understood in this way due to any formal anointing. Jesus was not a formal priest. He did not have the requisite formal credentials for that title. Besides this fact, the priests were consistently the targets of the prophets' attacks of moral outrage. They were a part of the problem. Jesus could not afford to have His message compromised by holding an official office, whether political or religious.

Jesus's authority is exclusively moral. Once again, Gandhi reminds me of Jesus. Jesus impressed Gandhi. The power of his leadership in India was moral. He persuaded people to follow moral principle more than a moral man. Gandhi was neither wealthy nor did he hold any political office, yet his moral character and moral courage attracted and inspired millions. Justice drove him, not ego. This man would impress Jesus. He might even say of him, as He did of the Pharisee, "You are not far from the Kingdom."[100] Jesus's leadership was based on moral wisdom, moral character, and moral courage. He expects His disciples to be the same. "If anyone would be my disciple, let him deny himself and pick up his cross and follow me." No one is a leader who expects people to be mediocre.

I am amazed at how focused the apostle Paul was on making disciples. His standard was incredibly high. He says, "For this reason we teach everyone and admonish everyone in order to present everyone *perfect* in Christ."[101] Again, he says that the equipping ministry of the church has the objective of bringing everyone to attain to the *"perfect* man, measured by

---

100 See: Mark 10:31–34

101 Colossians 1:28 ὃν ἡμεῖς καταγγέλλομεν νουθετοῦντες πάντα ἄνθρωπον καὶ διδάσκοντες πάντα ἄνθρωπον ἐν πάσῃ σοφίᾳ, ἵνα παραστήσωμεν πάντα ἄνθρωπον τέλειον ἐν Χριστῷ·

the full measure of the stature of Christ."[102] He says of Christians that those gifts are most to be desired that most edify the body.[103] He ranks the gifts as "First apostles, second prophets, third teachers, and then . . ."[104] After a compelling digression into the character of love in I Corinthians 13, Paul picks up his argument about the higher gifts saying "earnestly desire the higher gifts, especially that you should prophesy."[105] Why is prophesying the "higher gift" that disciples should desire to acquire? It is, in my view, precisely due to the fact that in the prophet, whether male or female, the moral standard of holiness interfaces with holiness of character. That is, one's moral leadership arises in virtue of one's moral character, not in virtue of one's formal leadership office. The question for anyone who would become Jesus's disciple is not whether she/he complies with some externally defined morality that is externally imposed, but whether it arises from an internalized holy character.

It is not sufficient, even if successful, that moral leadership depends merely on complying with some externally defined moral standard, although one surely does exist. Aristotle understood this and wrote in his *Nichomachean Ethics* that a just society exists only to the extent that it trains people to be just. He understood that this objective could only be met by a regimen of training that makes virtue a habit. Habit is the product of discipline. Aristotle believed that people should not become leaders in the city-state until they had become sufficiently educated and disciplined in applying virtue to themselves before applying it to the affairs of society. For Aristotle, politics is the place where virtue in men guarantees a just society. Aristotle and Jesus would have had a very interesting exchange because he and Jesus seem to realize the same thing, namely that *doing what is true, right, and good depends not on just laws but on just people, for the righteous man needs no law.* A moral message delivered by someone morally tainted loses its moral force. Jesus's moral message was morally forceful because it was not only morally defensible, but also because a holy man delivered it.

---

102 Ephesians 4:19 μέχρι καταντήσωμεν οἱ πάντες εἰς τὴν ἑνότητα τῆς πίστεως καὶ τῆς ἐπιγνώσεως τοῦ υἱοῦ τοῦ θεοῦ, εἰς ἄνδρα τέλειον, εἰς μέτρον ἡλικίας τοῦ πληρώματος τοῦ Χριστοῦ

103 I Corinthians 14:4, 5, 12

104 I Corinthians 12:28

105 I Corinthians 14:1

Edwards Brothers Malloy
Thorofare, NJ USA
May 21, 2013